Red Eagle Speaks

A Book of Wisdom

Native American Creek

Chief Red Eagle

Speaks Through Psychic Medium

Riz Mirza

As told to Oriah Miller

RED EAGLE SPEAKS:
Riz Mirza As Told To Oriah Miller

Published in the United States of America.

Journeymakers, Inc. Publishing

www.JourneymakersPublishing.com

This book is a work of non-fiction channeled by
psychic medium Riz Mirza.

ISBN-13: 978-0-9841142-6-9
ISBN-10: 0-9841142-6-2

Printed in the United States of America
12 11 10 9 8 7 6 5 4 3 2 1

**William "Red Eagle" Weatherford, (1765 – March 24, 1824)
was a Creek (Muscogee) Native American**

One of the most noted figures of the early 19th century lies buried beneath a stone cairn in Baldwin County, Alabama. Born "William Weatherford," he was also known to later generations as "Red Eagle," a noted Creek warrior. His war name was *Hopnicafutsahia* or "Truth Teller."

This book is wonderful. Each time I have had the privilege of hearing Red Eagle speak, he has touched something deep inside of me. My heart swells, my eyes water, and I feel truly loved. Riz is the 'real deal,' and Red Eagle lifts you up to a higher dimension of pure love. As if that were not enough, his wonderful sense of humor will keep you in stitches. Love, laughter, and truth...what else could one want?

— Lisa J. Ensign, angelic intuitive and healer, Yucca Valley, CA

Red Eagle is more than wise. He is compassionate. He gently presents profound insights into our personal lives while often using humor to lighten the load of our collective human experience.

— Scott Wells, actor, writer, filmmaker, Santa Monica, CA

Honestly, I find the readings of Red Eagle so profound. I'm in awe thus far. His teachings have touched upon the depths of my soul.

— Vivian Fabian, R.N., Los Angeles, CA

What you channeled was strong medicine - a bit bitter tasting at first! My life has improved because of your information and I have been doing what Red Eagle told me to do: Meditate and write.

— Napoleon Reyes, Los Angeles, CA

One of many favorite quotes from Red Eagle: 'There is only Love. Keep to your path, don't be so hard on yourself, do what you love....live with passion and take care of your body.'

—Zie Ramirez, Huntington Beach, CA

I am excited that Red Eagle is willing to share his messages with the rest of the world and give everyone a chance to open their minds to the universal teachings of a true legend and Native American chief with this book.

— Chris Thompson, young entrepreneur with an MBA, Palm Springs, CA

Riz's Dedication

To my love, Oriah, for being my co-pilot on this incredible ride on the wings of Red Eagle. I love you.

To Alex Murray, the beautiful trance channel in New York City and the spirit guides he channeled for awakening me to discover who I am and my purpose.

To my dear friends: Violette Shah, Kia Colton, Therese Clinton, Tommy Tejeda, Cheryl Merz, Vishaka, Sunita, Linden, Naina, Dr. Larry Sosna, and Srinija, Dennis Strahl, Rob Kaye – for always believing.

To my family: Bhaijan, Raja, Nabil, Taj, Nilo, Elena, and Yasmeen.

To Red Eagle: I don't know what to say to you, except I look forward to when we meet on the other side. Thank you for being my friend.

Oriah's Dedication

Thank you to my children, my mom, and stepfather for being a constant support and loving me through every stage of development and allowing me to share with them these pearls of wisdom that I have so abundantly received.

Thank you to Riz for being my knight in shining armor and proving that fairy tales do come true after all. I love you, my Twin.

And to Red Eagle: To you I find no words for the guidance, love, and wisdom you shine on me and how you help me transform my life...I love you.

About

Red Eagle Speaks: A Book of Wisdom offers powerful insights and flexible, clear, and practical life teachings. Psychic medium Riz Mirza has the rare gift of being able to receive communication from a being named "Chief Red Eagle" who lived on Earth more than a century ago.

This book was dictated word for word by Red Eagle through Riz and told to Oriah Miller over a series of thirteen nights. Oriah documented this collection of spiritual guidance and compiled it into this book.

Red Eagle's message is a powerful one of self transformation and evolution. His teachings give insight into the ego, shifting perspective, and overcoming fear, while awakening the love within all of humanity. Red Eagle's language is simple, provocative, and easy to understand by all no matter what "level of spirituality" they are on.

When you have pure unconditional love for yourself that means you don't have baggage from the past. And that means that you don't have the insecurities that were created in your mind from other people telling you that you're not good enough. That means that your body does not hold onto the past traumas that are over now. That means that each day is a new beginning, truly.

Everything you put in your mouth can be tasted for the first time and everything your eyes gaze upon can be perceived with interest and intrigue, that every conversation you have with every person you meet has your full attention with no judgments.

It is not to mean that you cannot decide that this is a negative or positive situation. If you are speaking to a person who is negative, of course you can decide by yourself: 'This is a negative vibration. I do not want it in my field of experience.' What we mean is that the interactions you have with people can be more spontaneous, can be more playful, like when you were a child before your parents told you to be cautious of others, suspicious of others. Now you can find the perfect balance of being open to the world and being sensible.

~ Chief Red Eagle
Recording of Red Eagle channeled by Riz Mirza 03/28/2011

Riz Mirza As Told To Oriah Miller

Foreword

Throughout the ages there have been revolutions and wars. Humanity now sits on the very precipice of the biggest leap in consciousness we've ever faced in our evolution. It's not only that we are being told this. We can feel it. And we are staring straight into the proverbial third eye of an inevitable spiritual revolution. We seek answers. We need solutions. We could use a map and directions. How apposite that someone, not just from some other mysterious dimension – a dimension unknown, unseen, and perhaps only cautiously sensed – but from our own past would come in now to help guide us through into our future.

When *The Seth Material* and *Seth Speaks*, which are regarded as significant components in the foundation of the "New Age," were channeled to psychic medium Jane Roberts beginning in the 1960s, many people embraced this information as definitive evidence of life elsewhere and beyond, and as proof that we are being guided, cared about, protected even, by something other than ourselves – by beings that refer to themselves as "spirit guides." While multitudes were, and continue to be enthralled by the entity, Seth, and the channeled material from Roberts, some shunned it. Some ignored it, and some proclaimed it evil hogwash. However, with the veil undeniably thinning more now between our world and the other realms, channeled messages from spirit guides are no longer regarded as an oddity, a rarity, or something to be looked at askance, but rather as comfort, reassurance, sage advice, and wisdom for all. Decades having long since passed, *Red Eagle Speaks* is the "Seth" for our contemporary times and beyond.

As with anything, when seeking the real truth of anything, we must use discernment. We must look to the "fruits" of something, and we must internally and individually decide what is truth for us and what is not truth for us. One thing is crystal clear in this sometimes muddy "revolution of spirit" that we are currently engaged in: We can sit immobilized on the edge of the red rimmed canyon and stare blankly straight ahead and off into the distance, perhaps afraid that we're going to fall into the cavernous abyss, or we can choose instead to fly…and soar…*like an eagle*.

— Dyan Garris, author, psychic medium, and New Age recording artist

Riz Mirza As Told To Oriah Miller

Table of Contents

Awakening you to the origins of the self, this chapter explores and revitalizes one's own self-awareness. By reminding you of your unlimited potential that is the natural state of your Being, you will see how your life sprouts from the seed of awareness.

What you see is what you get. What you don't see or envision for yourself is what you do not get or manifest for yourself. Your perceptions are your key to unlocking your future and changing the effects of your past.

It seems all of existence is in some sort of balanced perfection and control. By learning to refocus our relationship to the ideas of perfection we can begin to transform and understand how we make our lives too rigid and unbalanced.

Many people feel that it is our similarities that we must celebrate. But in the new era of human evolution on the spiritual level, we can discover the profound wisdom and compassion in learning about, rejoicing, and respecting our differences.

Another word for "gift" is a "present." The present moment is a special gift. When we learn to appreciate the beauty of where we are in body, mind, and spirit in the "Now" we can embrace the journey instead of waiting endlessly for the destination.

*Chapter Twelve....*The Body 126

How we feel in our bodies and how we feel about our bodies is a huge part of our culture. Yet we know as individuals little information is available about how our bodies actually function "psychically," or how our bodies hold unexpressed emotions. Developing unconditional love for our bodies is a daunting task. When we remember and realize that our true state of being is wellness and vitality, we begin to master the mind-body connection.

*Chapter Thirteen....*The Beginning 137

You are at the beginning of your life, no matter where you are and how old you may be. You are in a constant stage of evolution with no beginning and no end. But for the purposes of this book, we will explore how your true beginnings are wherever you start your journey and how to really master your life.

Oriah's Introduction

Over the last year and a half I have had the privilege and honor of watching Riz Mirza trance channel Red Eagle and other spirit guides at our weekly private and public channeling gatherings. I sit, like usual, in the back of the room mostly, wiping the tears from my eyes as I watch dear fellow human beings sitting in a semicircle conducting conversations with a guide that is not in our dimension.

I have witnessed the exuberance, the joy, the thrill, and the tearful release of people hearing things they have waited their entire lives to hear and didn't know it, or things they never wanted a soul to utter about them. I have witnessed mothers being reunited with their children who have "crossed over" and adult children feeling the satisfaction of feeling completion by having their unanswerable questions answered from their loved ones, their mothers, fathers, sisters, and brothers on the other side through Red Eagle.

Every day we get emails and messages from people whose lives were profoundly impacted by the teachings and wisdom of this Native American chief that lived hundreds of years ago. It sets them on a new course of life, a new perspective. And they can now see a new direction for their life's journey.

That brings me to Riz, whose eyes, lips, mouth, and body make it all possible. The seamless, symbiotic relationship between these two "light beings" brings a warm glow to my heart. The selfless act of Riz, as he rests comfortably in a dream-like trance, allowing Red Eagle to speak through him for more than five hours straight at our longest held circles, shows his devotion to bring peace and understanding to people...it will forever inspire me.

Now Red Eagle's wise teachings have been dictated, transcribed, and dedicated to you in this book. This has been a long time coming for all of us and we are honored to have you join us for the duration of this book to experience your own soul journey.

— Thank you, **Oriah**

Riz's Introduction

Ten years ago, if someone had told me that one day I would be publishing a book by a Native American chief who lived over a century ago and who would "borrow" my body while I was in an unconscious trance to give psychic messages to people on a regular basis around the world, I'd have thought they were crazy.

At the time, I was an artist and a musician pursuing a career in New York City, doing my best to make my dreams of superstardom a reality. One evening, I attended a gathering at the home of Alexander Murray. Alex was a trance channel. He could leave his body at will and spirit guides would speak volumes of wisdom through him. Everyone sitting around the cozy living room would get personal psychic messages too. All of the messages were delivered with such love and respect - all very positive.

I was so excited waiting to hear what my spirit guides would say to me. I had several questions ready, mostly about my musical career and when I would "make it." When the spirit guide got to me, he paused and took a few moments to begin. I thought to myself, *Wow, they know I'm gonna be a rockstar!*

Well…the spirit guide basically ignored my musical dreams and simply said, "You are a channel."

I thought to myself: *Right. I'm a singer, and I channel songs…*

The guide was pretty curt with me, I thought, when he came right out and said my band wasn't going to "make it" and that my life was to be on the "spiritual path." I had no clue what he was talking about and I left that night thinking of the better ways I could have spent my money!

I barely slept that night. I couldn't stop thinking about how profoundly accurate Alex's messages were to every single person and their amazing reactions to his readings. Yet, I felt - or tried to convince myself that I felt - that his message to me that I would be a channel was way off. I ran from this psychic message for nine years. I will fill you in on all the details of my story in a future book. For now, let's just jump ahead those nine years to the present.

Today I am a psychic medium and I trance channel just as I was told I would. Many different spirit guides communicate through me, teaching me so much, and allowing me to give a lot of people a lot of peace of mind and love.

Red Eagle introduced himself to me in 2008 while I was in deep meditation. And I will never forget the first time I heard his voice. It was so wise, strong, and peaceful. I know you will feel the same when you read his words. When he speaks to people, he has a huge presence and heart, not to mention a great sense of humor!

His English is broken at times and we kept that aspect in the book as much as we could. There are no typos that we know of, so please remember that the way it is written here is exactly the way he speaks. My partner in life and in business, Oriah Miller, sat across from the good chief for thirteen nights recording his words and transcribing them with great care. Together, we are embarking on a lifelong mission to spread his teachings to you and throughout the world.

Like Red Eagle says: *It's all about co-creating.*

With love,
Riz

Red Eagle's Introduction

Hello, I am Red Eagle and I will speak. Where do we begin? We should begin in the moment, for that is where change must always begin – this moment. Everything is here and now in this particular moment…this moment when you are reading this book, not the moment before or the next moment that your mind is jumping to, wanting to know what will be in the next chapter or the next page.

What will you get out of this book? I have a better question for you: What will you put *into* this book? What will you bring of yourself to this book? It is a co-creative effort. Everything is created by what you bring of yourself to it. Maybe you think Red Eagle is writing this book. I think *we* are writing this book. In this moment, what is between you and this book? What is there that stands between you and understanding, feeling, absorbing the concepts and the words, the heart that is beating in between the words and between the lines?

There is only one thing in between what is in this book and you. *You.* You stand in the way of yourself from learning something, from experiencing something because there are always two of you. There is the one 'observing' and there is the one 'doing.' Sometimes you are the observer – you say: *I cannot believe I just did that, I cannot believe I just said that.* So, you are observing and also doing at the same time. But much of your life flashes before you so quickly that time passes and you feel you have not truly done much with this life.

You feel that time has passed you by. It came and went so fast. Now you are here and you feel old even if you are young. There are many questions about 'what is time?' The greatest answer that I have to give you is how you make it. What you do inside of it, what you bring to it.

Who am I? Who is Red Eagle? Maybe you are reading this book because you think Native American chiefs are very wise. Let me tell you, there were very many chiefs that were not very wise in my time. I have had many physical lives. I am a spirit, a pure essence like you. But I am unfiltered, unbridled – and in my purest state. I AM. And through a very interesting and peculiar process I am able to come through what you call 'time and space reality,' and speak through the body of this young man called Riz Mirza. He is the person whose body I am speaking through. He is a channel. The woman recording my words is called Oriah. Riz and Oriah make my words available to you.

It is like when you are watching the television, you watch a channel. What is a channel? It is the particular frequency position of the unit. The television that is picking up a particular frequency that is flying through the air, and so, like the television, Riz is 'tuned into' my frequency. A frequency is measured in wavelengths. That is why when you understand someone, you say you are on the same wavelength. You know what it is like to be 'tuned in.' When you meet someone who is tuned in, you say, 'Oh, it was a pleasure to meet that person. It was very exciting, they are so tuned in.' People pay a lot of money to speak to people, to work with people, to hear people who are 'tuned in.'

For some of you, a person who is a channel is a strange new concept. Why? Even you, who is reading this book, have channeled. Many of you – I should say all of you – have experienced a time in your life when you have said to yourselves: *How did I say that? How did I know that? How did I do that? It was beyond me. I don't know where I got the strength from. I don't know what made me think of that. I had told that person so many things about their life, when they were telling me a problem, I had the solution. My mouth was moving. I did not know what I was saying but I felt energy when I was doing it. There was great intent and great wisdom in my words.* We will say you were channeling. You were tuned in. You were dialed in.

Who are we? We are your spirit guides. When you dial into us, we answer the phone. You can say we don't let it go to voicemail. And we always have the time for you. In your very business oriented world, your production oriented world, your results oriented world, your quick results oriented world, your regimented world, your scheduled world, your disciplined world, is there bliss? Those structures, are they working? You might say: *Yeah, the trains are arriving on time, the tracks are holding the train. They are on schedule. Planes are landing. Babies are being born with all sorts of complicated machines around them, to make sure everything is alright.* Regimented and safe, yes, all to avoid disaster when it is not in the structure or the process, or when the regimented schedule happens, then people call that 'disaster' or 'big trouble.' Many times throughout history, you reveal how incredible each of you are by working through a disaster. But it no longer has to be the only way to become your best. There is more.

When you are working with the energies that you refer to as 'metaphysical' or 'spiritual,' it is a whole new ball game. It is not about structure. Not in the way you see it. The artist, the creative people of your time, of all times

– they know what we are talking about. No artist likes to be put into a structure or into a time schedule. That is very painful for them because they know of creation in a very different way than others.

It has been said that all people were born as artists – creative. But as soon as the judgment comes on them about what they are doing, if it is not beautiful or creative enough then the child is discouraged, not encouraged. They are disempowered, not empowered…and so you are killing creativity in your young. It is everywhere.

You say only certain creative people will fit into your regimented world – your quick results oriented world. And when you have time to reflect on these things, once in a while, you feel saddened. You talk about the loss of innocence.

Self love. That is a term nobody wants to hear. It has become cliché that you have to 'love yourself more.' That solution is not enough for you. Spiritual lessons that tell you to be more compassionate, to respect the Earth, to love one another, to believe in yourselves, to let go of your past, to let go of your fear, to be appreciative and grateful for the many blessings you have received. You disregard these teachings and you say: *I have heard that before. I hope that this book by this dead Indian chief will tell me something new.*

Ha! You want something more, something that will move you. While the world, the planet Earth, is flying through space, spinning around, tilting back and forth, breathing and pulsating with countless amount of creatures and living things, moving through space around the ball of fire that you call the sun, and you are sitting there thinking you are not moving, while everything else moves. You are on the planet, flying on the course of a cosmic path. You people wonder why things don't change fast enough. And we guides wonder why you don't change fast enough.

So here we are in this moment, at the beginning. That is all we have. In this book I will talk to you. I hope you will hear me. Everything that I will tell you is for you, specifically *you.* Do not think of the fact that there are millions of others reading these words. How do you know this book wasn't meant really for you – just for you? I want you to hear and to read these words in this book like I have written them just for you and you alone.

Let us begin.

Chapter One

Seed

You begin your life as a seed. Don't you find that interesting? Have you ever thought about it? You are a seed that gets implanted into something else – a living being. This Earth is our mother. Your mother – you plant seeds into her, don't you? And when you are implanted into the mother you are nourished. You begin your life, *Seed.* That is what I will call you now. You begin your life, *Seed,* in darkness. No sounds, not really. No light. The seed is implanted into the soil. That is all that. . .

Only the placement, nothing more is done to the seed. It is only placed into an environment where growth occurs. As it is sleeping – if you think it is sleeping – let us say for this conversation, *Seed,* you are sleeping. In the dark, silent environment that you cannot see outside of, because you are a seed and you are closed, it is rich with nutrients. It is a large mass, pulsating, living, nutrient and you are nestled in it. Somewhere outside of you, outside of that environment of nutrient rich soil, or womb, there is rain. There is sunshine. And there is *shit! Ha!* Magical things...all three of them.

They are true symbols of creation. Let us talk about the rain. Where does it come from? It is mostly a mystery to most people walking around. I believe they tried to tell you where it came from when you very young and were in school. It had something to do with the oceans and the temperatures of the water rising up and then coming down again. Nature knows how to recycle. Man only learning now.

But you know, recycling is a very natural part of the human experience. What do you think *shit* is? It feeds the ground, it feeds the seeds that grow into maybe a vegetable or a tree with fruit, and the human being eat it, extracts what it needs, and then excrete what it doesn't need. Animals too, it goes back into the Earth and feed the seed and it goes over and over again. You may find it humorous. And it is! It is wonderful that you are a part of this process – you, the Earth, the tree, the fruit. It is a beautiful circle of life. And it can continue for eternity. And so the rain comes, the ocean goes higher, and it continues over and over and over again.

Let us talk more about shit. Because many people out there feel like life is shit, that life has shit on you. It is a very popular word. It means many things, and you can say, "Some bad shit happened to me." You experience something very good and you say, "This is good shit." You have an accident and you say, "Shit." You win a lot of money and you say, "Holy shit." I think shit is very holy because it is a divine process.

Let us talk about an example of when life shit on you and what you can do about it. This will also be a very practical book for you. In fact, I hope this is the ultimate practice book for you. You are going about your life, suddenly some crazy shit happen. Life has brought you a lot of shit. And you are standing there looking at this shit in front of you and it smells really bad. Your first instinct is to make a face and to run, to get out of there because you don't need this shit, and you leave.

You look for greener pastures. By the way, they are green because of you-know-what. So you are somewhere else, and the shit is there, and along comes a farmer. He is walking by and he says, "Holy shit!" He has a big smile on his face. He gathers the shit and he get to work. Maybe sometime later you return and where there was shit before, now there is a garden. The farmer is sitting there smiling and winking at you and you are hungry. He has a lot of vegetables and fruits that he made with your shit. He knew what to do with it. Every sign of life is in nature.

There are solutions to your problems in the examples of nature. Many of you respect the Native American people because they are very in tune with nature, respecting, working with - using it properly. You can do also, you can understand *natural process* - how nature work - so that you in your modern regimented world can achieve more peace and move forward. The farmer knew how to use the shit. He knew that its properties were rich in nutrients. And he did not care about the smell. In fact after a while he kind of started to enjoy the smell because that smell meant money to him. He connected the dots from A to B to C to D to E to F. And at the end there is food. There is nourishment.

But many of you, my friends, who are reading this, you get stuck at the smell of the shit. It is so offensive to you. That is why you say, "I cannot deal with this shit."

There are not only physical cures for what ails you in nature, the scientist and doctors know the cures for your disease must be in some plants somewhere, so they are searching night and day. But there are also spiritual cures in nature for how to live better that is found in nature. I will give you another example. I will talk about the snake. Oh, it seems nobody likes the snake. Anywhere you go in the world, mostly, snake is something to be afraid of. For good reason. It could kill you very easily.

But most snakes are not poisonous, only a few are. Let's talk about those ones, because those are the ones that bring you fear. Let us imagine that you are bitten by a snake that is poisonous and its venom is coursing through your veins. All the cells in your body are on high alert, condition critical. Sirens going off inside your body, that there is some poisonous fluid about to reach the heart. The venom works very fast, my friend. You will sweat, you will shake, you will tremble, and you will ache. You will begin to panic and the world will seem to go kind of fuzzy. Maybe you will see double or triple. You will fall to your knees. Perhaps your life will flash before your eyes.

Everything – things that you should have done or should have said, or shouldn't have done or said – flashes in an instant into your understanding, your realization all at once, and you become certain that you are about to die. It is killing you, this poison. It is destroying you. And so you look to the sky. Every last drop of who you are is crying out with all its might: *I want to live!*

But what will save you? There is no cure for snake venom, other than one: The antidote, the anti-venom. You have seen it in movies and stories and television. It is the quest for the antidote. Can they bring it in time to save this person? It is in the jungles of life.

You are dying and the antidote contains the answer. What is it made of? Do you know? The antidote is made from the venom, think about that. The cure is in the poison. *The thing that is killing you contains that which can give you your life back.*

It is time to get your life back. They took the venom, extracted it from the serpent, and through the venom, through a *process* and was able to make the anti-venom.

There is a spiritual lesson here, my friends. Do not run away from the problems and the challenges. Do not run away from what seems to be poisoning you emotionally, psychologically, spiritually, and especially mentally. You must go in there and extract the cure. It is why they say that which is inside you but does not come out, will kill you. That which is inside you and comes out – will *save* you.

Perhaps you are reading this book because many things in your life right now are not going the way you want them to. You don't feel good. You do not need to complicate your expression of how you feel. You can start off by saying, "I don't feel good." It is the basic expression. It has to come out. You are so used to telling each other you are fine. "How are you? Hello, how are *you*? I am fine. I am fine. I am good." It is rare that someone really telling you the truth.

Most people really don't want to hear if you are not fine. You want to know why? They will say, "I have my own problems, why are you telling me?" So nobody is being honest with each other. It will be a huge leap in human consciousness before you are able to have discussions about how you really are feeling today. But everyone is always in a rush to get somewhere so they don't want to hear anything other than, "I am fine."

Sometimes it takes someone to ask you, "How are you *really?*" to get a little bit of an answer out of you because you are always off rushing to answer your cell phone. That is a very incredible device you have invented so that you could always be reached. How do you always like always being able to be reached? Is it wrong to be unreachable sometimes? We will talk about this further later on in the book.

There are many fascinating things about human beings. How about their personalities? How they think. One thing that is interesting to Red Eagle is that you are always looking for something new but you also don't want to change.

You always want to experience something different and new, and yet you like the old because also it is comfortable. You do not want to throw away certain things because they are old and comfortable, or maybe not so comfortable. But it has been so long that you don't even realize that it is not so comfortable.

It is like when you have an old pair of shoes. You are walking around in them for so long and they are dirty. People tell you your shoes are dirty. Maybe they have holes in them, but you know when you put your foot in there it feels good, you feel normal. Then maybe later on when the shoes are falling apart you need to buy new one, and you go to buy the new shoes, and now there are so many. Because it has been so long since you have bought a pair of shoes or sneakers, that the style that you are wearing, maybe they don't have it anymore.

You are standing there in the store with all the sneakers and you are wondering: *Where is the one that I used to like to wear?* Then the salesperson maybe says to you, "Oh, we don't have that one anymore." Now you are forced to get something new so you try to find something that is like the one you used to have. Then you get it and put it on, maybe the salesperson convinced you to spend a little bit more money.

You put on the shoe or the sneaker and you get in it. Oh, it feels very different. It is like the old shoe, but you realize you are far more supported - forgive the humor - the new shoe has more "soul." You put both on and you walk around. You feel like jumping, you feel like running.

You look at the old pair and you cannot believe you were wearing those before. And you say to the salesperson, "I will take it and I will wear them home." It feels so good you don't want to take them off. Because you get used to the old patterns, you get used to the old shoes. You wait until everything is falling apart for you get something new.

I don't want you to wait like that anymore. Your life is too short. I want you to refresh your perspective. Don't wait until there is nothing left but holes in your shoes. Your old shoes are like some of your old relationships and friendships that no longer support you, that are full of holes. Maybe even your foot got bigger so it no longer fits.

You need an upgrade. *Why do you wait for everything to fall apart to make something new?* You are smarter than that. Perhaps you think you are done learning, is that it? Many of you once you reach thirty-years old, that is it - you have learned everything you need to know. Many of you have children by the time you are thirty, so now you have to teach them and so you pretend to know. You say to someone, "Stick to what you know." *Really?*

You should be on your knees thanking the heavens above that the people you respect and admire and call your heroes did not think that way. They did not stick to what they knew. They stuck to what they did not know. They pursued what they did *not* know. They had a drive to know more, to experience more. They knew that knowledge put into action would become wisdom. They knew that having that wisdom and to share it with others would give them a feeling of great satisfaction.

You are here to teach each other and to learn from each other. You never stop evolving. Some of you learn in school about evolution.

Whether some of you believe it or not, do you think you are done? As a species? As a planet? You are not done. The creative force of the universe is never done. There will always be more. You climb one mountain and there will be another. You climb that one, there will be another. Then you will want to go into the valley, and then maybe you will want to go deep into the ocean. It is the nature of what and who you are.

When you say, "I need to get back to nature to balance myself," do you even know what you are saying? It is not that you just want to be around the trees. It is that you are returning to your natural state of being. Every cell in your body when you are in nature is responding to what is around you.

Could it be possible that your body has wisdom? I am not talking about your mind. I am talking about your body. Your body is smart enough to take the nutrients out of food and excrete what you don't need. You don't use your brain for that. It is not thinking: *Hey, this part of this food I do not need and the rest I need.* It is the body that has the wisdom, but the body needs your help.

Your body is pure wisdom and your mind sometimes gets in the way of that. That is why you put things into your body that is not so good for it and your body tries to adapt. It struggles. It tries to stay in balance. You are putting bad things in there, it tries to get rid of what is bad and tries to get whatever is good in there. But over time your health suffers. The wisdom of the body is supreme, but your mind affects it.

Let us talk about food. You learn to think certain foods taste good. What you are fed becomes part of your diet. As a child, some children will refuse certain foods, and some children will refuse some other foods and you say, "My baby doesn't like spinach but she loves pears." It is because the baby is fully experiencing the food. The body knows what it needs. But since the baby is not in control of what he is eating, because many parents are force-feeding the children, the child and the child's body is forced to try to make the best of the situation and extract the most of what it can to please itself, to nourish itself.

So now the baby only wants sweet things, and so the sweeter it is the more the baby wants it. So now you give him very salty things, same things happen.

The child is innocent to it and so it grows. Then every time the child cries you give it something sweet or salty and the child becomes quiet. Now the child gets older and the child says, "I want what it is sweet."

You get angry and say, "Why are you always asking for sweet? How you can wake up in the morning and want something so sweet?" It makes you angry. But it is you who have given the child that.

Now you have to begin a new kind of discipline from the food because if they continue to eat that way they can develop many illnesses. It is normal, it is natural. This is not complicated science, my friends. We are talking about the basics of life that you know. We are searching everywhere for the answers. How to lose weight? Is it that complicated? You eat less and move your body more. Eat fresher, healthier food that comes from the Earth and drink more of the water. Is that so complicated?

Nobody gets fat eating cucumber or broccoli or carrot. But then you say, "I do not like those things. I cannot eat it. It doesn't taste good to me." So now you have to go back to the basics. Don't you? Why in your busy life, you do not stop to question *why* you like what you like? You are a thinking person. None of you are dumb, not one of you.

Only many of you have not been given a chance to learn the most basic things, yet somehow you still know them. You know in your heart that if you eat less, you will lose weight. You know in your heart that if you eat more fresh food, you will be a healthier person. You know that if you think more positive thoughts, you will be happier person. You know that if you forgive, people will also forgive you. You know that fighting doesn't lead to anything good. You don't have to be a rocket scientist to understand that, as they say, or a brain surgeon or a heart surgeon to understand what is in your head or heart.

But you may say right now that Red Eagle is doing brain surgery and heart surgery on you. For me to do this, you have to have an open heart. My brain surgery is to open your mind - that is the surgery. There is nothing else. My heart surgery is to open your heart. There is nothing else more to it. I want to open your mind and I want to open your hearts more than they are. There are some of you reading this book and saying, "I know that. I know these things that he is talking about." Knowledge is nothing. Wisdom is everything. Because: *Wisdom is when you put it into action.* You know that old saying?

Those of you who know what I am talking about, and those of you who *think* you know what I am talking about, who say, "I have already heard what he is talking about," you should pay more attention right now. Like I said, this is written just for *you.*

Do you think they build houses differently than they did before? Do you think they build a chair differently than they did before? Mathematics, do you think it has changed? Do you think the formulas have changed? You still put a seed into the ground and the animals still shit on it. The clouds still rain on it with help from the oceans, and the sun still shine on it. That has not changed.

To cut the piece of wood, so that it is equal in measure with another piece of wood so you can build a strong home - that has not changed. Yet there are so many homes that look so different. There are so many plants that look so different. But the seed do not look any different, not very much. The rain is the same, the sun is the same, and the shit is pretty much the same. *Same shit, different day.*

Music. There are basically sixteen notes or so, but how many songs are there? How many songs are there in the world? Billions of songs from centuries ago until now. Billions of songs with the same sixteen notes rearranged and yet, mostly all of the songs sound different.

Different styles of music, different rhythms, different languages, different melodies, harmonies, tempos, flavor, feel, resonance.

Different, but from the same basic ingredients. Even if you are the most advanced musician, you still have to play the same notes the beginner musician has to play. You are only playing it in a more complex pattern, so you think.

Advanced musician playing the same notes as the simple musician playing: *Do Re Mi Fa So La Ti Do* - that is what you people do. Backward and forward over and over again, different combinations. That is the same as spiritual teachings, and your life. The spiritual teachings are the notes. The songs you make out, it is your life. The seed grows.

Chapter Two
Perception

Do you feel that there are circumstances beyond your control? That they are affecting your life in many negative ways? Circumstances in your job, your relationships, your relationship with family, your health? Circumstances politically in the country you live in? Circumstances in the environment all around you and the environment within you? Have you ever thought about that?

There is an environment inside of you – yes, of course your thoughts and emotions – but what about the internal dialogue? What about that circumstance? What about the old tapes that play in your head? The ones that say over and over again to you: *It's not going to work out. It's not going to happen to me. This is my life and I am stuck with it. No one understands. Life is hard.* These are just some of your thoughts that are a part of your internal dialogue.

Like the dialogue in a movie you watch, one character says something to the other and the other says something back. It is like your negativity is one of the characters and you, the sensitive one, are the other character who is suffering, having to listen to that negative character always talking at you. You are aware of this. I know you are aware of this because you seek to comfort yourselves.

It is a natural quality in every human being to want to comfort themselves. Unfortunately, many people comfort themselves with things that are not very good for them. Too much eating, too much drinking, too much fighting, too much stress, but people do those things to comfort them - even the things that are bad for them - because at the moment they feel good to do. They do comfort you. It is temporary, but it seems to be good enough for most people.

You work all week long and you have to put up with people and situations that are very stressful. People that you do not like, systems that you do not agree with, and you are not heard and you are not recognized. It is physically also draining. So when the weekend comes and you want to relax, you want to be comforted and you call that "having fun." Maybe some of you like to drink alcohol. That comforts you, it relaxes you. It makes your mind more at ease, to a certain extent of course, because if you drink too much alcohol, your mind is no longer at ease. Because all of your inner negativity and your demons come to rise up and comes out of you and you say things to people that they do not like and later you regret.

Some of you channel this frustration that you are accumulating during your week into physical activities. Maybe sports, exercise, sexual activities, and those are also comforting temporarily. It is like blowing off steam. Then Monday comes and you go back to your same old routine. And this becomes the cycle of your life. In between, perhaps you have a relationship, you get married, and you have children, maybe you get divorced, you meet someone else. That becomes the structure of your life. It becomes monotonous, doesn't it? Because it seems nothing is changing. You are getting older but not necessarily better. The old body does not seem to do what it used to do.

Even if you are young right now, you who are young and reading this book, you are understanding what I am talking about. Even you at times feel like your body is getting older though you are young - not as energetic and full of vitality like it used to be. How much of this has to do with your mental state, your lack of energy? That is a big complaint for everyone. Lots of companies making lots of money, making lots of products that they say it will give you lots of energy. There seems to be a preoccupation with the term "lots of." Everybody wants "lots of" something, yet it seems that it is never enough. I will talk about that later. That is a strange phenomenon.

For now let us talk about energy. What is energy? Does it sound like a silly question? Everybody is supposed to know what energy is. In school they teach you different types of energy. Electrical, kinetic, static - I am not talking about those. I am talking about how you radiate. Haven't you ever noticed people who radiate? You walk into a room and you can see there is energy around the person. Even a person who is being quiet, it is not necessarily only someone who is talking very loud or wearing bright colors. You can sense the energy. All human beings have this sense within them. Some of you call it a sixth sense. A sixth sense is sensing energy in a person, place, or thing. A person does not even have to be moving and you can feel their energy when it is high.

How does that happen? Are they eating different foods than you? Maybe. But there are some people who are eating worse foods than you and they have better energy than you. Or let us say *more* energy than you. But of course in your society, more is better. So more energy equals better energy.

When you run out of energy, your body goes to sleep. Don't you find sleep strange? Have you ever stopped to think about it? What is sleep?

I want to play an imagination game with you now. Imagine if you were a space alien and you didn't really eat food or water - you just existed maybe by light or something strange like that. You came to Earth to observe the creatures and the humans, and you noticed that every ten or twelve hours after these human beings and creatures have been running around and talking and doing and singing and creating and laughing and fighting and playing and working and eating and drinking, and suddenly they start to slow down and stop completely.

They fall to the ground or lay down, and it looks like they are dead. They close their eyes and everything in their breathing and their body systems slows down. For eight to ten hours they don't move, not really, but they are breathing. You try to open their eyes, maybe wave at them, but they don't see you. You talk into their ear, they don't hear you. You pinch their hand, they don't hear you. It is almost like they are dead. Where did the energy go?

Sleep is a very fascinating thing. All of your scientists know many things about sleep but they still don't know what it is. How it work, why it work, why does it work to regenerate your cells? They cannot measure energy in the body. They can measure almost everything, but they do not yet have instrument to measure energy of different people.

They cannot place ten people on their table and use an instrument and tell how much energy this person has. They have to ask the person, don't they? "How much energy do you have?"

The person will say, "I have a lot of energy."

The next person will say, "I have so-so energy."

And the next person will say, "I have no energy."

The doctor or scientist will have to believe them and try to find out why. They will go into the blood and say, "It is an imbalance of nutrients." And all sorts of reasons they will find. But they cannot tell who has the most energy without asking.

These are very simple things to think about, but they are deep. And I ask you to think about them because it is the simple things in life that are the most powerful. Your mind, your thoughts, and your emotions are the main factors affecting your energy on all levels in your life.

Let me give you an example about how your thoughts and your perceptions can change your physical energy. Let us say that it is very late at night and you have worked a long day. And in your day, there are things that have bothered you. Maybe there is a person, if you think of that person you get agitated. Maybe when you are walking home there is a person always talking to you and they never shut up. You just want to get home after a long day but they keep talking and talking and it aggravate you.

Maybe every time you come home, you go into a store. And in that store there is a person that you are a very attracted to, a person who makes you feel good inside just by the sight of them. But you are too shy to approach them, too shy to perhaps become closer to them romantically. So you only go into the store, buy a few things and you walk out after saying "hello" and "good-bye" and "thank you."

You walk home thinking about that person, maybe you dream about being with that person. And as you are walking home, you can feel how tight the muscles in your neck and shoulders are. Now you need a massage but you cannot afford it. Maybe you should go home and have a drink. So you are home and your phone rings, and it is a good friend who say to you, "Are you sitting down? Because I have some exciting news for you."

You yawn and you rub your neck and say, "Make it quick, I have to go to bed and wake up early to go to work tomorrow."

Your friend says to you, "What if you do not have to go to work tomorrow after what I tell you?"

And you say, "What?" Maybe you are interested right now. What crazy thing is your friend going to tell you?

Your friend says, "I had a very rich uncle I did not know about and he left me ten million dollars. You have always been a good friend to me and I don't need ten million dollars. I only need five. And I would like to share it with you. Do you think you can use five million dollars?"

You are holding the phone and you think it must be a joke, and you tell your friend, "No way! I can't believe it."

Your friend says, "I am serious. Come tomorrow. I have to go speak to the lawyer and sign the papers. It is tax free money and I am going to give it to you."

And you say, "Oh, my God."

Your friend says, "Yeah, thank God, miracles do happen. Now you can do everything you wanted to do. Remember you had that idea to start that business? Well now you have the money to do it.

You say, "Wow, I can't *believe* this!"

Your friend says, "Believe it. Meet me tomorrow at two o'clock."

You hang up. Now it is 11:00 PM and you are starting to walk around your house and it is starting to hit you. You are about to receive five million dollars.

Everything is going to change! You don't need to be at that job anymore that you don't like because you can start your own business. Now you can buy new clothes. You can go and talk to that person in the store and maybe ask them out on a date. You can start to do many things that you have been putting off. You lay down in your bed but you keep thinking of many things, and you are having many visions of success. You are seeing a life that you never thought was possible. You can't sleep...*too much energy!*

Through some miracle that was happening without you knowing - behind the scenes - it has now come forward into the foreground of your life. It is miraculous. You get up and you look in the mirror and your heart is beating faster and you begin to laugh, thinking about all the things you will do. Suddenly a certain confidence starts moving through your body. You feel your prayers have been answered. Somebody somewhere was finally listening to you and your soul's desire. You realize that it is not that late. The store is still open. The person that you like is still working.

So you hurry up and take a shower, you put on very nice clothes, you go down there, you get some flowers, and you go in and you say to the person with a big smile on your face, "Hello, I hope you had a nice night. I have always wanted to talk to you, here are some flowers for you. Would you like to spend some time together?"

The person sees your radiant smile, the energy is so bright around you, and they say, "Yes, I would love to."

You feel like jumping for joy. On the way back home you look on your cell phone and you see that you have received a message from your boss - the one who is always on your back telling you they need to cut your pay. They forgot to tell you that earlier at work. For all the work that you do at that job, you cannot believe the nerve of them to cut your pay.

You decide to take a stand. You call the boss and tell them, "You don't respect me or my efforts and I deserve better." You tell your boss all the things that you have been doing - how important you are to the job.

The boss cannot believe the confidence and the clarity in which you are speaking. You are not angry - you are not *too* angry I should say - but you are angry enough to speak these words, speaking the truth of who you are and what you need and deserve. Then your boss says, "I will think about this."

The boss begins to sense you have something else going on. You have the five million dollars, you don't need that job. So you hang up and you are radiating more energy than before. You go up into your apartment and you turn up your music and you begin to dance around.

While dancing around, you remember a friend or a family member whom you have been quarreling with whom you need to forgive, or perhaps you need to ask for forgiveness. You feel life is too short, you want to start anew and forget the past problems. So you do call and they are sleeping and you say, "Hello, I need to talk to you. Life is too short. Many good things can happen, miracles can happen, I know this to be true. Let us put the past behind us and start anew. I love you, I am sorry, and I hope you forgive me and I forgive you too."

You hang up and you realize you have not eaten dinner. You go to fix something to eat, but you realize you don't want that heavy food you always have. You would be happy with an apple and a glass of water. So, you take a bite of the apple and you sit at your table, smiling, thinking about tomorrow. What a good friend you have to bring you the good fortune of tomorrow's five million dollars. The phone rings. Very happily you answer the phone and your friend says, "Are you still awake?"

You say, "Are you crazy? How can I sleep after the great news?"

And your friend says, "What great news?"

You laugh and you say, "About tomorrow. About our amazing gift your uncle has left us."

There is suddenly silence on the phone. Your friend says, "Oh no, don't tell me you believed what I was saying! I was only joking with you. There is no money and no uncle. Sorry…did you really believe such a crazy story?"

Your heart stops beating, it seems. You are in shock. "Tell me the truth right now, were you lying or telling me the truth?"

Your friend says, "I am sorry, I was only playing a joke." You are furious and you throw the phone across the room.

Now you are sitting there in your home and you don't know what to do. You are furious and your friend has lied to you. You are in disbelief at the events that have occurred over the past several hours. You feel betrayed and angry. Suddenly your agitation reaches a very high level, and you don't know what to do with yourself so you begin pacing back and forth. Maybe you are throwing things around in your home. What a stupid cruel joke to have played on you. What was the point? Suddenly you realize, "Oh, my God, my job! I called the boss and I said many things that probably made him angry. I will be out on the street without a job!"

You nervously wonder if you should call your boss now and apologize. "It's too late," you say. "I will have to face the music tomorrow and maybe I will tell the boss I was drunk or something and I did not know what I was saying or doing." Then you remember the person you met at the store. How will you explain that one? Now you suddenly don't feel so confident. You don't even have the money to go on the date with the person. Of course it was all too good to be true.

You need to calm down, so you open the refrigerator and there is the heavy dinner you avoided earlier. Maybe there is a pizza or some other fattening food and you sit down and begin to eat it. But you don't even taste it. You are just "inhaling it," as you say.

Your foot is tapping as you are eating, your eyes are staring into space, your blood is boiling. Even though you are feeling all of those stimulating feelings, exhaustion is creeping over you, deep in your bones too. So you finish your meal, maybe you have a glass of wine to help knock yourself out of this bad feeling. The exhaustion is so heavy, you have to drag yourself to your bed, literally, where you collapse, falling into a world of strange and disturbing dreams. Eventually the night passes and the morning comes.

You are groggy as you hear the telephone ringing. "What?" you answer.

It is your friend, or the person you *thought* was your friend, up until the cruel joke they played on you. They say to you, "Hey, good morning! I am outside waiting for you for half an hour. Where are you?"

And you say, "Why? What for? Waiting for me?"

Your friend says, "Stop joking around. We have to go pick up the money."

As you are lying there in the bed, you stop breathing. You stare at the ceiling without blinking, holding the phone in your hands.

You hear a voice saying, "Hello, hello?"

You are not responding and you say through your teeth, "What did you say?!"

He answers, "I told you, you have to meet me, we have to go pick up the money. What you think? – you were not going to get the money I promised? I was only joking again. Of course you will have the money. Why would I play such a cruel joke on you? I am your friend. I have always been your friend, you can trust me."

Now you don't know what to feel. You are in a state of emotions that are changing rapidly. You are going from anger to hope to confusion to resentment to excitement to fear to…suspicion. Then you end up feeling like a zombie, not feeling anything at all. You begin to have hope again, because your friend convinced you that it will all be okay, and you shall receive the unexpected abundance, the gift that is coming to you.

Why do I tell such a long story? What is it that I want to communicate to you? I want to tell you do not let yourself be a puppet emotionally and psychologically to what anyone else tells you.

In this scenario, because you believed you were going to be fine and taken care of and supported by the Universe, you were able to break through certain barriers, obstacles, challenges in different areas of your life. You were able to stand up for yourself in this scenario with the boss. You were able to honor yourself and approach a person you were interested in. You were able to respect yourself and your body by not wanting the heavy meal late at night.

You were awakened to the infinite energy that is flowing through you at all times because you were not tired anymore when you found out the exciting news for the next day, because you believed. All of this, because you believed you were getting that money. Then when you found out you were not getting it, your energy dropped and your anger increased.

You began to regret your actions. You began to second guess and third guess your friendship with that person. You began to say to yourself: *I know I shouldn't have trusted.* Your perceptions can make you a puppet. But how do you use this toward your advantage? There is a way. Try to see your future as a bright one. Try to imagine the Universe has many gifts for you that are a beautiful surprise that seems to come out of nowhere.

Try to find a way inside of yourself to fully expect better results than what you have hoped for. Try to *feel* what it would feel like to have those things. Because when you were told by your friend that the money was yours, you believed it. You felt it came from an authority. You perceived it as fact. What you perceive as fact will become fact.

But we are talking about emotions. People who do not believe they are loved are very lonely. If you ask the people in the lives of the lonely person if this is true, they are not loved, they will always often tell you, "No! That person is loved very much. I am that person's brother and I love this person very much. I am this person's friend and I love this person very much. I do not know why he or she feels they are not loved." Many people will say they love that person, but if that person does not believe it, then their entire reality is dark.

My friends, everything is in your perception. You have come to a point in your life now that you have to start to pay attention to this. Nothing else is working, don't you see? You have had temporary fixes for your problems. When you change your perception of events, you change the event. This is a remarkable fact. May I prove it to you?

Everyone has experienced death in their lives. They have experienced a loved one dying. When it is first occurring in your life that a person has died, it is extremely painful. Many of you question life itself, many of you question God. You cannot understand how the Universe can allow a person to die in such a way and leave so many people sad.

Over time, certain things begin to change - your perception - and perhaps years later you are able to say to yourself with much less emotional feelings, that your mother, father, brother, sister, or friend had died. Maybe someone one day asks you how many parents you have and you say, "I have one parent and the other parent died ten years ago." You are not crying when you say that statement. Why not? The reality is the same - they are dead. Or is it? Your perception has changed. You begin to understand the cycle of life and death, or shall I say, simply the cycle of life. Death is a part of life, not the opposite...that is a heavy statement isn't it? That it is a part of life, not the end of it.

In this book we will begin to redefine certain words and concepts that you have taken for granted. Your perception has changed. Some of you think years after the person has died that it was better that they have not lived this long. You have insight into certain people. You say that person was on a path that you could not see that it could be resolved here on Earth. Then there were people who die in tragedies. That is very difficult to understand.

We will talk about all of these things at a later time, but I think you catch my drift. Some of your perception changes over time, you begin to release the emotional charge behind your feelings and you become calmer and more peaceful. You begin to say, "My loved one is now in more peace. They are on the other side." And your heart and your soul is comforted.

There is an understanding, because it took a certain amount of time to get to that place of balance, so you are unaware that your perception has expanded. Some hope, no longer believe in God. Some people when they lose a loved one, they believe in God even more. Our discussion here is not a religious one. Our discussion here is only for you to examine how you have been thinking.

It is time for you to observe how you have been thinking. I do not care if you are only fifteen years old reading this book or fifty-five years old reading this book - there is something here for you. Because the very fact that you are reading this means that there is something that needs to be more properly aligned in you, and that is one of the more beautiful qualities of the human beings. It seeks for something outside of itself to help it become more of its true self. It is a beautiful quality. Be proud that you are seeking to expand yourself. Be happy that you are trying to understand more about yourself. Be pleased with yourself that you are seeking to better yourself.

Your thoughts are mostly in the past or in the future. People will tell you "Do not think about the past, you cannot change the past." I am here to tell you my friend, you can. You can change the past. How? How is that possible?

When you change your perception of the past, you will change the past. Let us talk about this simple example. And once you understand the simple example, you can create even more complex examples in your mind to observe, and it will benefit you greatly in the present.

Many of you have experienced setbacks, difficulties, little tragedies that affected your life. At the time, it seemed very restrictive in ways. You maybe broke a leg and you could not go to work and make any money, so you got behind in your bills and you suffered greatly. Emotionally, it is a lot of stress and it lasted for a period of several months. So you had to work even more to make up for lost time, and you say, "What was all that for?" And you are now bitter about it.

People have experienced similar situations, and many people who have experienced something like this say, "You know, but at least I got to rest in bed while I was healing and I had time to think and get some perspective." Many people after tragedies are grateful because they realized although some of the things were feeling negative at the time; it created many positive effects that were felt later. It was not to mean that only through painful experiences you can grow. You can grow through delightful experiences as well.

Why do you say, "No pain, no gain?" There have been plenty of times there have been pain and no gain, and there have been plenty of times there has been no pain and a lot of gain. You have learned a lot just by watching pleasurable things. You have learned a lot by watching two babies playing together and laughing. You can observe their behavior and you can learn something from it and it can make you smile. Now you are wiser because of something that was pleasurable.

Let us get back to this changing the past business. Many of you who have been through a relationship that have caused you pain – maybe marriages, maybe business partnerships that went sour. The person that you once got along with, you no longer get along with and you say you cannot believe that happened to you, you are suffering from the effects of the past in the present. You resist the lessons you have learned.

When you resist the teachings that the experience is providing for you, even though it is painful, you create even more pain in your life because you are bound to repeat those mistakes. Experience alone does not bring wisdom, my friends. Only deep and profound insight into those experiences can provide you with wisdom. Some people say, "Oh, I had to learn my lesson so I had to experience that." I would say that is pretty much true.

But do you have to keep learning this lesson? Repeating it in a new situation? Do you have to keep attracting more situations like that? Now we are talking about attracting. Do you attract the same thing over and over again or are you a victim of circumstance? People always say, "Why does this keep happening to me?" Of course the cliché is you have not learned the lesson the first time. You have heard this before. You have heard it so many times you do not want to hear it anymore.

But you don't do anything about it. That is a big core problem. That is what is at the root of all of your discomfort and dissatisfaction of your lives - your resistance to becoming your Higher Self. Every aspect of pain in your life lies in your resistance to becoming your Higher Self.

What is your Higher Self? Some of you have known this term, but how much do you relate to it or think about it? The Higher Self is the fully expanded and expressed version of you. What does that mean? It is the best version of you. It is the version of you - body, mind, and spirit at its peak; the superhero version of you, the perfect version of you. I don't say the perfect person - I say the perfect *version* of you. You...free of fear, you...free of regret, you...free of sorrow, you...fully open to the vitality and the resonance and the sheer life force that you are.

The Higher Self makes every move based on its pure unconditional love of itself. When you have pure unconditional love for yourself that means you don't have baggage from the past. That means that you don't have the insecurities that were created in your mind from other people telling you are not good enough. That means that your body does not hold onto the past traumas that are over now. That means that each day is a new beginning, truly.

That everything you put in your mouth can be tasted for the first time, and everything your eyes gaze upon can be perceived with interest and intrigue. That every conversation you have with every person you meet has your full attention with no judgments. It is not to mean that you cannot decide that this is a negative or positive situation. Of course you must decide that.

If you are speaking to a person who is negative, of course you can decide by yourself: *This is a negative vibration. I do not want it in my field of experience.* What we mean is that the interactions you have with people can be more spontaneous. They can be more playful like when you were a child before your parents told you to cautious of others, suspicious of others.

Now you can find the perfect balance of being open to the world and being sensible. Think about so many things in the past that were so painful when you were experiencing them. Now you see, if it was not for those experiences you would not have met that person or did that thing, or gone to that place that led you to that, that led you to that, that led you to that, that led you to a new kind of happiness, and that kind of advancement, that kind of growth, and that kind of joy, and that kind of deep understanding. Now here you are, all because of those very troubling experiences at the time.

If you choose to be wise now, my friends, you will see that you can change the past. No matter how traumatic it was for you, you are still here, you still have hope. There is something so powerful within you. It is a built-in mechanism. The fact that you still try, every single day to move through your day productively in some capacity, shows that you have hope.

When you say you are hopeless now, I don't believe you. When you say to me you are hopeless, I cannot accept that. What I see is a person who is so wonderfully sensitive to the world and experienced things that were not matching your expectations. Your feelings were hurt to such a degree that you shut it off - this connection to hope. Because your hopes were dashed by so many experiences, it is natural my friends. But think about this, if you were truly hopeless, you would not be reading these words now. You do have some hope. Right now, with these words, you have this moment...you will always have this moment to begin to make a change.

Chapter Three
Control and Balance

Let us talk about control. It is wise to be in control as you drive your car. You place your trust in the pilot of an airplane to be in control. You expect your government to be able to exert control over the infrastructure and the economy. You expect your teachers to control a classroom. When you first begin to go to school, you truly begin to learn what it means to control yourself. In fact, you are reminded to control yourself at every turn as a child. Why?

Why do they want you to control your behavior, which when you are a child, seems very natural? Completely natural. You don't know you are doing anything wrong. When you are a child you don't know what "wrong" means. Those around you, who are your guardians, tell you to control yourself. *Do not do this or say this. Control yourself.* With their words and actions, they are trying to control you. So they are trying to control you and they want you to control you. Your entire existence now has a new angle.

So as you are being, doing, thinking, creating, the aspect of control is very prominent. When you watch a sporting event like in the international competition, the Olympics, you praise the athletes that are on the balance beam. You reward balance. You praise those athletes that show the most control, who are able to move their body, or not move their body at the precise time with the precise amount of physical effort, strength, flexibility, and balance.

Those qualities seem to be very important to the world when they are watching the Olympics. The one who shows the most of those qualities is declared the winner. He is declared the best. He is now respected by everyone. Strength, flexibility, balance, poise, form, energy, and even style are very important. How does control fit into all of this? It is very apparent you must control everything about yourself to be able to achieve very high levels of skill in those areas. It is simple math for you, but what about your own inner life?

In relationships? If everything in the outside world, for you to move forward through life, is about controlling yourselves, why is it in your relationships you are trying to control others? You want people to behave a certain way that will please you. You want them to think and feel a certain way that is in line with what you believe so you feel more comfortable interacting with them. Think about it.

But it is more than that. There is nothing wrong with tribes of people who believe in the same thing to be together. Of course the problem only arises when they feel they are better than another group of people. It seems this has been a problem for every generation. Socially, politically, sexually, intellectually, one group feels they are better than the other and then they want to control others.

Yes, think about it. They want others to think like them so they themselves feel stronger. Strength in numbers. You are seeking strength because you lack it. It is very important for certain religious people to have more people believe in what they believe. They feel more right and it validates them. Speak to certain religious people who have converted other people, they are very proud of that. What does it do?

It is a very complicated topic, the matter of control, because you must have a certain amount of it and then you must not have it at all.

When are the times where you must not have control? Some people say in love there should be no control, in passion there should be no control. Do you really believe that? Think about your love relationships. If you don't control your passion, it could consume the other person. If you control your passion too much it can destroy or at least damage the happiness of the other person.

You are seeking balance in your lives and many of you do not even know it. You are seeking to learn, to control your issues of control. Imagine that. That can be very confusing. It is like saying, "I don't like to procrastinate and I will stop procrastinating tomorrow." *Ha!*

It is an exercise in futility. Governments are trying to control other governments. You see what that has resulted in. We suggest that it is time to think of a different paradigm than control. We mean simply, is there a way we cannot use the word control when it comes to relationships - relationship with others and with yourself?

Let us go back to when we were talking about your childhood. Mostly, when children do not know how to express what they are feeling in a manner that is acceptable to you, you feel that this child needs to be controlled. But what really needs to happen is you need to hear what they mean, not what they are saying.

That is what you have to do throughout your life if you intend to truly understand every situation that transpires that causes you pain or confusion. In the moment when something that is challenging you in your life is occurring, the other person is having an argument with you because they cannot control their emotions. They say words that are harmful to your sentimentality and ego.

How do you begin to learn what is meant behind what they said? Wars are started because of words. Maybe two things need to happen. Maybe one person needs to control their words or maybe the person listening has to have the patience and detachment to try to see beyond the words and hear the meaning, the intention, hear the meaning, the expression of the other person. It is up to you to do one or the other or both.

When some people are accusing the other person of something sometimes they say, "What a jerk." You say much harsher words than that, but for this book I will say the word *jerk*. "You are a liar, a cheat." What is behind those words? When you say, "You are a jerk," what you really mean is, "I am very hurt by your actions." When you say, "You are a liar," you are really saying, "I was vulnerable to trust you. I felt close enough to trust you. I am happy because I am in a relationship of some sort of trust between us and it hurts me that the trust was broken."

When you say, "You are a cheat," you are saying, "I had high hopes for our interactions. Because of the honest qualities you displayed to me before, I believed in you and I didn't think this would happen."

You see, that cannot be said by most people because that means you have to be vulnerable. And to your society vulnerability is the same as being weak, and weak means *bad* to you. But you don't even know what it even means to be weak. If you were to pick up a very thin flower, or a blade of grass it is very thin, do you feel it is weak? Maybe you are not seeing the beauty and the strength in it. Beauty and strength are two qualities that when they are together they are Divine.

Beauty without strength cannot survive, and strength without beauty will be despised. Look at the leaders in the world, if they were strong but had no beautiful qualities, they are disliked by many people. But if there were some leaders that were only soft and beautiful, they were destined to disappear.

The great ones had strength and beauty together. Watch one who has lasted the test of time, man or woman it matters not - we are talking about the essence of the person. Those great people whom you considered to be influential to your people, do you think they tried to control others? They did not. They asked the world to become more balanced, which is all they ever wanted from you. If you focused your attention and energy on becoming more balanced in your life, you won't have to worry about control.

You lose control because there are some areas of your lives that you are not being expressed. You are off balance. If you work too much and do not play enough – out of balance. If you play too much, and do not work enough – out of balance. If you talk too much, you're out of balance. If you don't talk enough, you're out of balance.

Life is about flow. The trees know this. The trees that bend and sway with the wind do not become very stiff because they will crack, they will break, and they will fall. The birds know when to go with the flow of the wind, the fish in the sea also. When you go with the flow, you release too much control and your life becomes better. When you release control, you open up the doors to pleasant surprises. When you release control, you allow the universal force of goodness to move you through life. When you release control of people, you let them find their way.

You let them be in the flow of life, you allow the Universe to handle it for you. You are not the controller and manager of the Universe. If there is a person who you feel is out of control and is creating worse and worse situation in your life, you must remove yourself from the situation. What keeps you there? *Control.*

Manipulation, it is a part of control. People will emotionally manipulate you to try to control you. They try to control you because they are afraid. They are afraid of feeling weak. That fear of feeling weak comes from vulnerability, and you would have to trace it far back into childhood, for most people, and you would have to find a time in their life when they were vulnerable. Vulnerability means you are open to possibilities.

Do you know it is possible to be strong *and* vulnerable? Oh, you have never thought of that – maybe you don't think it is even possible.

Little boys are told to control themselves when they are crying, not so much with little girls. That is why many of you say, "He cried like a little girl." And that is a very big insult to say to a man. If you don't believe me go try it right now to some man, say to him, "You probably cry like a little girl." But isn't there nothing sweeter than a little girl?

Why do you tell your little boys not to cry? Why? Why does it bother you so much? Why don't you teach them that sometimes it is okay to cry, but crying too much damages you – and it does, my friends. If you are depressed and crying every day it is not doing you good, believe me. There has to be balance.

To achieve balance you have to start to try to understand yourself, and to understand yourself you first have to begin with compassion. You have heard it said so many times, by so many people, to have compassion. Your religions teach you that, world leaders teach you that, spiritual teachers teach you that – but it is so difficult, is it not? It is far easier to show compassion for your friend than to yourself. You would never judge your best friend the way you judge yourself in your mind.

You are not pretty enough, or handsome enough, or skinny enough, or smart enough, or talented enough, or strong enough. Those are the things that you say to yourself, but you wouldn't say that to a person that you truly care about. Why is it okay to say that to yourselves? Then, if you start to tell yourself that you are those good things, another part of mind kicks in and you say: *Don't be so conceited. Don't be so arrogant. And don't try to build yourself up so much.* We are not talking about becoming arrogant – again the word *balance* comes up.

Your mind becomes obsessed with the word "control." When you tell the little boy to not cry, he processes this information pretty much only in one way: *It is bad to cry because crying makes you look weak.* Now he has no way to release the emotion because crying is not acceptable to you. He will not receive positive life energy from anyone around him if he continues to cry in that way.

So now the little child has to figure out when they are in pain, how should he or she express themselves. Some begin to retreat within themselves; they do not say anything at all. Some react violently. Very few channel that energy into creative, productive things. So the first step of becoming a "control freak" in boys and girls begins.

Those same tapes that play inside your own heads of you not being good enough in a variety of ways, begin to play in the young child's mind as well. And so after a while, the whole world is like this.

There are differences amongst nations, if you go to the East certain countries, the men there are softer. They seem more feminine to you, for those who are in the West. They show their affections for one another as men more openly. And to them, you seem very hard and unapproachable.

Those who try to control you have succeeded, for now you have no spontaneous interactions using your common sense. In fact even your common sense has been formed due to their control. When you were children you did not have these judgments on yourselves. The world needs compassion more than ever before. Why? Because more than ever before, all of you are getting a chance to know each other all over the world through technology, through travel. The world is opening up – getting closer together – seems like the world is getting smaller.

You will need more compassion because you will meet and see more and more different kinds of people with different life experiences. And you will have to show compassion and they will have to show compassion to you to make a more balanced world.

As you guide your vehicle on the highways of life, don't grip the wheel so tight. Hold the wheel with a relaxed feeling, not too tightly or too loosely. We want you to have a pleasant enjoyable ride, not one in fear that accidents will happen. When you release excess control, a more organic type of successful result will occur. This will give you great pleasure. You will delight in the results. The word "delight" is a beautiful word. It is different than "pleased" or "surprised."

To be delighted by something, I feel is very special, maybe because the word "light" is in there. It made you feel *light*er, it shed *light* on the situation – you were de*light*ed to see something. When you control too much, it robs you of feeling de*light*. When you control too much, it robs you of feeling the "Light."

Chapter Four
What is Normal?

Sometimes you say to your friends, "I don't feel normal today." You wish to feel normal, to feel the way that you did before when things didn't seem out of balance. So maybe "normal" means "balanced," but is your life balanced, really? When you say it is "normal" maybe normal to you means you don't want to be disturbed by any new circumstance. You are used to a certain way of being and you want it to always be like that. But that it is not the nature of life.

That is not the nature of the universe. Your scientists are saying your entire universe is still expanding, and you know very well that you are a part of this universe, so it is impossible that the universe is expanding and you are not. Or is it possible the universe is expanding, life is expanding, and you are resisting? You have free will and you also have stubbornness. Although some of you are too stubborn to expand at the same rate as the universe, to evolve that way, you use your free will to slow everything down. Some of you say, "Hey, stop the world from spinning, I want to get off."

When things are happening very fast in your life, like big changes… it is very important for you to understand, it is the process, a signal, a sign that your life is going to the next level. So you get caught up in the pain and the trauma from the current troubling environment. You are resisting it. And in the middle of it you say, "I want it to go back to normal." And yet you know you cannot stop whatever is happening.

Your resistance is causing you even more pain, because you like to be in control. We want you to flow with what is happening around you at all times. Of course nothing that happens to you is there to destroy you. You say, "Everything happens for a reason." True, but it takes you so long to understand that, you suffer and suffer and suffer in your misery. And after, you give yourself some solace in the words: "Everything happens for a reason."

You don't know why a loved one has died, you don't know why you have lost all your money, or your friends, or your home, or your health. You say, "Everything happens for a reason." But yet your feelings about that situation are very negative or bitter. Because in your ideal world it would not be happening, and so the basis of your understanding is that pain and not feeling "normal" is bad.

Probably none of you ever remembered the first time you cut yourself and you bled. You can remember certain times, probably not the first time that it ever happened, when you were very, very little. When you cut yourself and your blood flowed outside your body for the first time, it was a chance for your body to do what it was made to do, what it has a built in mechanism for. How the blood will dry, how the skin will start to protect itself and regenerate itself? It is built in, in all of you. You might say it was a good thing that you scrape your knee as a child and bled because it was your body's debut into awakening its self-healing.

Things got activated within you, that is what I am saying to you. The trauma of falling activated the healing nature in you and you became stronger.

Your body created the scab where there used to be a cut, and then the scab also disappeared. Could it not be true for the spirit, for your feelings, for your understanding of what is happening around you that is also causing you pain? What is the self-healing that happens then, when your heart is broken and your feelings are hurt? Or when there is any kind of negative emotional experience?

Does "normal" mean things never change? That things are dead, have no energy, don't move forward? How do things move forward? Often times, it is through conflict, or confrontation, confusion, contact. Through that kind of opposing forces – their extension pulling one way, pushing the other – for you to realize how truly adaptable you are, that you have it inside of you to become better. Everything that happens to you that you consider to be negative is for your betterment.

You are on a journey here, on this planet with all of these people who are around you. They are your classmates. Every one of them is experiencing pain, pleasure, struggle, triumph, loneliness. These, you might say, are the required courses here in this school. Some of you keep taking the same courses over and over again! Apparently, "heartbreak" is a very popular course here on your planet. I want to help you. I want to help you realize who you are and what you are.

There is no such thing as "normal." You have a code of behavior amongst your society that defines what is normal, what is acceptable, what is tolerable, and what is good, by a certain standard. This creates a lot of problems. Of course, on one hand, it creates a stable structure for your society but if someone is not like the rest of you in certain ways, you feel that the person is not normal and that is a bad thing. Unless that person becomes very successful being abnormal or weird, then you consider that person a genius.

Look at that Walt Disney. Before he became so famous, he only had a drawing of a mouse. He had a dream of making his own city, his own kingdom, all starting with a drawing of a mouse that could talk. Do you not think that people thought he was not normal at all? They probably thought he was downright crazy, but now he is considered genius. He has left a legacy. Because he did not adhere to what would be considered *normal.* He was himself. You reward individuality only when it is very successful financially in your society, but you condemn it when it is not successful. You say, "That didn't succeed because it was too weird, too abnormal."

Then somebody succeeded very big and you say, "You have succeeded because you are not normal." Which one is it? Do you fail because you are not normal? Or do you succeed because you are normal? I want you to give the word "normal" a rest for a long time. I want you to think about becoming who you truly are because there is a "normal" inside of you that has never been seen.

You have been spending your life in a series of reactions to all the things in your environment. And so as you do all those things, and you have your life and you have your ups and downs, there is a nagging feeling in all of you that something is missing. You cannot be with yourself.

It is very difficult for many people to be alone. I am not talking about just being alone – am talking about being alone and being happy. Because so many people are alone and sad or have settled in their hearts and minds to be alone. They feel they really don't have a chance to have a lot of love in their lives. I am not talking about those people, I am talking about can you be by yourself and happy, just to even sit in a room? Sometimes for some people to even sit for five minutes alone without talking on their phone, without moving their limbs, without reading a book, without doing something, is very difficult for them.

It is because they are not present. They don't know how to be in the present. If anything should be "normal," it should be knowing how to be in the present, like the animals. Like everything in nature. Like babies, that is why you are fascinated with them, with all of these things... because they are truly in the present. I would like you to think of being "normal" as being in the present.

I would not like any of you to have your lives go back to "normal," then I would be doing a disservice to you. For I see in all of you so much potential waiting to burst. But because of fears and insecurity you don't go forward unless you really, really have to, so you fall behind. You start to get old before your time, you get tired and jaded, and then that becomes the "normal" state of being.

You are a unique individual. There is no doubt about that. It is only in your mind that you think that all people are the same. Yes, of course, they have similar challenges, similar basic needs. And collectively you as a people, as a nation, as a planet have agreed that certain things are important and good. You all believe that freedom is good, that to be peaceful is good, to be in love is good. These are global values and desires.

What about some of the people who seem to be on a destructive course? It seems that they do not want any of those things. They only want to cause trouble, why can't they be normal? You will have to learn to accept that everyone has their own path. It does not mean that you have to share the path with them. It does not mean that they are allowed to hurt you or your society. But their role, the roles of each of you to each other, is of a teacher. To be able to through your interactions, provide an environment where all the individuals involved may become better. That they may benefit from what arises from that interaction for destruction of what used to be called "normal."

Many of you live in fear that you will be cast out if you do not act "normal," that if you start to think differently, speak differently, feel differently, express yourself differently, that you will be ostracized from your community. I am not talking about destructive behavior like hurting others, taking advantage of others. That is not what I am talking about.

Many of you don't pay attention to your tastes. You are afraid to change your style; you wear something different and the person says, "Why are you wearing that?" You start speaking differently and they say, "Why do you speak like that?" You change your taste in anything at all and they say, "Why? Why? Why?" Maybe they will make fun of you for that, they will say you are pretending to be something you are not. So there is a lot of pressure from your so called "community" that you stay "normal." Translation: *Don't ever change.*

Sometimes someone says to you: "Don't ever change." And you take that as a compliment. I think that is a curse. Change means that you are alive. Growth is change. But many of you are not confident that the change can be lasting, that you can maintain the change.

Many of you feel that you don't deserve the benefits of what will come to you if you truly change, and so you give up. You give up your dreams because you believe it can never happen. When you believe something can truly happen, naturally your efforts will be apparent to you and to everyone as being in the right direction to manifest what you desire.

Your body has wisdom. You break a bone, it knows how to heal itself. There's nothing the doctor can do except put a cast on your broken arm and tell you to rest and allow yourself to heal. They cannot make the bone grow faster because they know the body has its own intelligence and the body knows what to do.

Your doctors and scientists have told you your cells are regenerating all the time. Every couple of years all of your cells have changed in your body. So it is the very nature of all existence that you must change. You cannot stay the same. Do not worry about being "normal." Find what is beautiful about you and others that is not considered the "norm."

Of course we are only talking about the non negative and non destructive qualities – finding the beauty in your individuality. So you go on about your daily lives, your normal routine, you wake up, you wash up, maybe you eat something, you talk to family or partner, or your cat or dog. You go to work, you interact with co-workers, and you come home. That is the normal routine, and now they are saying – psychologists – that ninety percent of the thoughts you had today were the same as yesterday. Not many new thoughts have been coming in and so nothing changes. You wonder why things don't change. It is because *you* are not changing. You are deciding to keep things at the "normal" pace and level and feel.

You need a big change in perspective. You need to do things differently if you want it to turn out differently. You will have to change the "normal" internal conversation in your head when you are telling yourself you are not good enough, or it is too hard for you, or that you are not beautiful or handsome enough, or you are not capable enough. You are cutting yourself down all the time – that is a big part of the ninety percent of the thoughts, the worries, and the concerns that are old. Every day start to work on that, start to say encouraging words to yourself, treat yourself that you are your most beloved friend.

You would never use harsh words against a friend whom you would only empower and encourage. It does wonders. It transforms lives.

When you decide to not be so "normal," you become more spontaneous. You start to become more present. You become friendlier, loving, funnier, and sharper. People will feel more alive around you. They will want to be in your presence more and you will bring out the best in them.

You don't have to change your job, or your friends, or your home, or any of those things to do what I am telling you. I am telling you to go inside of yourself and as you change the way you see things, the things you see will change, and you will never want to have that old "normal" life again. It will be pure happiness in every moment. Even when you are miserable, you will still be happy.

At the same time, because the happiness will be coming from the understanding that whatever you are experiencing that is making you unhappy or miserable, is there for your benefit. That extra perspective allows you to move through the situation with more grace and with less damage.

The happiest older people are the ones who are present and are ready to experience new things every day and are connected to the love they feel in their heart. They have let go of the fear of death and they pay more attention to their love of living. Get out of your head. Get into your heart.

Chapter Five

Being Present

How much do you worry about mistakes you have made in the past? How much of your time is spent going over it in your mind, repeating it, seeing the same scenario, hearing the same conversations, confrontations, remembering the pain, feeling the distress? Much of your time is spent repeating that over and over and not really coming to any conclusion that can help you in the long run. Stirring up old feelings, anger, sadness, bitterness, regret – and like a dust cloud it swirls around you. You see nothing but grey. It does not mean that you should not talk about your problems or reflect on what has happened in the past. Reflection, contemplation, truth seeking – that is different.

Do you feel you are your past? I am not meaning to say that the path that got you where you are today should be discarded. I am talking about the mistakes that you think you have made. The ones that make you say, "Oh well, you cannot change the past." There is a way to change the past of course, by changing the way you look at it. But you know people – they get caught up, distracted by things, entertainments, and the day to day responsibilities of life.

Often you feel in life there is no more time to think, that there is no more time for contemplation, there is only work. Then you have to have a vacation, a break. Have you ever thought of why you really need a vacation? Of course the simple answer is you need to get away from it all.

But what about this cycle of work, work, work, and a little bit of play...then work, work, work? It seems to tire everybody out. It seems to be exhausting to the spirit. It becomes very monotonous. Routine is different, monotony, another matter altogether. When things are monotonous, you don't even see what can change, what is new, what is evolving. You become blind to the normal everyday things.

Your surroundings, the people, the tasks, they don't seem new – they are old. They don't seem to bring you any kind of challenge or excitement, or joy and every day it is the same thing over and over. And so you need more and more distractions. Yet inside you still want to connect to each other more and more. There is something in your spirit that wants to reach out to another, longing for a connection. It seems that all the ways you are trying to connect to each other, certain loneliness prevails. You avoid spending time alone.

Spending time alone and loneliness are very different things. When you spend time alone, you are spending it. You are not wasting it. You are doing something valuable, productive for your body, your mind, your spirit. It seems many things are lost today that were very popular in the older times. Not too many people have hobbies anymore. There used to be a time you had stores called hobby shops. Do you remember that? Now no more. People are distracted with their technologies.

Maybe technology can be a hobby for you. I understand that. But in the technology you are trying to reach out to someone else. On your Internet it is all about your connections – to be seen, to be heard – but from the privacy of your space where you sit alone. You want to broadcast yourself but you want to be alone when you do it. It is not a group activity in that sense.

It doesn't start as group activity. You are alone when you go on your computer, and you feel like you are in a group. But it is controlled by you. You can remove yourself from the group when you want to. That is not really a hobby. Many of you go to exercise to improve your physical condition, to relieve stress, to create peace in that regard – that is a creative activity.

I am talking about the quieter times, when there is less noise around you. People don't seem to like that. They want to avoid that. Because when there is less physical noise around you, you become more aware of the noise inside your mind. That is when the thoughts become deafening, like thunder. They are like a storm in the sky of your spirit. You want to connect to something. This feeling is very common for people all over the world now. They are not getting it from their relationships or their careers or religions.

You know when you are a baby, you don't need so much interaction? When you look at babies, you feel they should be playing with you, but you know, they are very happy in their cribs. They are so happy to be alive, to feel; they feel the electricity, the vibrations running through their bodies. They can feel their own auras. They can see another person's auras; they see a light around everything! That is why they are never bored.

Then as you get older, you want to connect and share your ideas, your thoughts and your feelings. You discover sympathetic interaction, to care for another human being. As you go deeper and deeper into relationships you start to become more aware of yourself. Now you have reached a point where connections between people are changing. You are kind of in the middle somewhere – that is what is happening across the planet. Through your technology you communicate with each other about many great things. And many great things have come of people getting together through this technology.

But you also know the great things that have happened around the world before you had it. Governments were changed, new techniques in medicine, art, music, science, all were accomplished before this amazing technology you have now. It is because of the spirit of the people that always finds a way to change the world, in ancient times and in modern times. But it seems you have less and less time in the day to do things that you really want to do, to continue with the interests you had when you were younger. You say, "I do not have time for that, where is the time? I cannot seem to find the time."

Then one day you will see that you have no more time, and you will have to question what your life was all about. Was it about paying bills, taking care of others? What about developing yourself? What about paying attention to your own dreams? What about getting to know yourself? Do you spend any time during your day getting to know yourself? That is a question not many people have ever asked you before. You are so busy learning about other people, you don't seem to want to learn about yourself.

It is not really your fault. Let us start with your human body. Most people don't even know what the organs are for. They cannot name their functions. They don't really know how to take care of it. You know the most basic things on how to take care of your body - how to clean it and to make sure you don't eat certain things. But you eat them anyway.

You are very incredibly resilient beings, but you have very little knowledge about yourselves. You leave it to the doctors or the scientists, and still people are dying of the same disease as before. Or they are kept alive with the medicines, but they are still suffering. You will have to start to know yourselves again and that comes with spending time alone with yourself.

To feel the energy of your own body - I don't mean the energy to run around - I don't mean that kind of energy. I mean the kind where you are sitting there and you feel the vibration of your skin, your flesh, your bones, and your heart. I mean time when you attempt to take in and quiet your mind and feel love for yourself, you check yourself to see how you are doing. You have to connect again with yourself and to do that you must disconnect from certain things that are distracting you.

What are these things that are distracting you? If you are not working, maybe you are watching TV. If you're not watching TV, you are talking on your phones. If you are not talking on your phones, you are talking on your computers. What about learning to play music?

In the old times there was a musical instrument in every home. It was not there to make someone to become a professional musician. It was there because the family and friends shared in the joy of singing together, joining their voices as one, sharing.

What about drawing a picture or painting? When you were children you drew pictures. That was your favorite thing to do. There has not been a child that does not like to draw a picture, and if you find one that does not like to draw, it is because an adult discouraged them from doing so.

All children love to sing until you tell them they don't sound good. Then they stop. And you do it to them very quickly at a young age. Maybe you don't say, "Hey little child, you cannot sing," but you do not give them positive encouragement if they don't sound perfect. So they stop, and begin to look outside of themselves. And when they look outside of themselves for validation or compliments from another person, it becomes a search that lasts a lifetime.

You have heard about meditation. Maybe some of you do it. You have noticed that people become more peaceful when they meditate, and many of you who are reading this book have been doing meditation for a long time. Many of you who have been doing that still are not leading peaceful lives. You have moments of peace during your meditation, it lasts, sometimes it doesn't, and it is different for everyone.

For those of you who do not practice mediation – do you know there is always something that you are doing in your life that is kind of like a meditation? You are trying to find a state of balance, of peace, of clarity for yourself. It is often done through some kind of activity. For some people it is to play sports on the weekends; for some it is to watch television. It is all, in a way, a search for peace of mind.

Even those who drink alcohol too much – although it is not a healthy way to do it, but they get something out of it – they have a few drinks and they are able to achieve what feels like peace. Some use drugs, some use sexual relations or shopping. All of these are some kind of therapy to help heal what is ailing you, to fill what is missing in your lives. It is a rather expensive way to do it.

When you learn to do meditation, it is much cheaper! You only have to sit somewhere in your home. Anywhere you are you can do meditation. Everyone can benefit from it. Meditation is a very powerful gift that will constantly rejuvenate you and you will never get old. Maybe you should turn off your phones for a day. Turn off your computers. Maybe only for a few hours you are able to do it, but it will help you.

Sometimes it is good to be unreachable, and others will know and accept your new boundaries. During this time you are taking care of yourself, and at first perhaps it will annoy them but they will learn from it. And believe me they will try it too one day. Because they will see how much more peaceful you are and actually how much more effective you are in your work and in your relationships.

It makes you do everything else better. So if you truly care about doing everything more productively, take the time for yourself. Don't wait until you have a vacation. If you work all day, try to step out a few minutes and breathe in the sunshine and the light. Stretch your bodies. Try to think of happy and humorous things in your life. Do not take yourself so seriously. And do not take your problems so seriously either.

Many of you have trouble sleeping at night. You are working very hard during your day expending your energy, putting it out there, and you come home and you need to unwind. But while you are unwinding you are realizing how tired you are. The day has escaped you and now the evening begins to do the same. Exhausted, perhaps you talk on the phone, on the computer, watching TV, and then you fall asleep.

There is no gradual shifting of your energies toward the time for when you are about to sleep. To reduce the noise for maybe the last half hour, you can have quiet time. If you have children, you put them to bed, and then you have quiet time. You really have no excuse. No one can stop you from taking care of yourself in this way. It is not difficult to learn meditation, but perhaps difficult to practice it. But it is never too late. You can do it anytime. You can learn it anytime.

It is very interesting, it seems people are more comfortable talking about themselves and their feelings and their preferences through their computer. You have people connecting on the computer through the Internet and revealing much about their lives and themselves. But to do in person, that seems to be very difficult for them. Some will say, "But I don't have the time." Why not? What are you doing? Oh, you are on the computer! There will never be a substitute for human touch, human interaction, in person, face to face, hand to hand.

While there is much to be gained from your technology, it is a tool like a hammer. It can be used to build or destroy. It is the same for all technology. It is the same for everything that is outside of yourself. To connect with another human being, to sit with them, and to not even speak, just to feel the energy and at home in the presence of one another, is a very beautiful thing.

Many of your younger friends cannot image life without their computers or communication devices. But they should learn to. All of you should perhaps have a day where you do not use any of these things. You play music, I don't mean listen to it. I mean play it yourselves. Maybe plant some flowers, learn to. Maybe read that book you have wanted to read. Or write!

Maybe wash your clothes by hand, so you care for your garments more from your heart. Maybe to sit with a friend, and look at photographs in an album that is sitting on your lap, to cook a meal together or alone. What about sitting alone for a little while and thinking about all the people that you loved or have helped you along the way, sending them beautiful positive energy? A day to be grateful?

What about seeing the planet Earth in your mind and wishing for everyone on the Earth, peace. What if every individual had inner peace? You would have peace. You would not have acts of terrorism.

What about everyone wishing peace for everyone else? What about sending love to the planet that you call your home?

It is time for you to make time for yourself. It is time for you to be alone with your thoughts and feelings. It is time for you to discover that you are in eternal spirit. It is time to live once again a peaceful, soulful existence. When you remove yourself from some of these distractions one day a week, or maybe once every two weeks, you will learn to appreciate the beauty of being you.

When you return to your distractions and technology it will be from a happier place, a more appreciative and grateful place. You will bring more back to your life. You may say to yourself: *But I don't know how to begin.* I say to you: *Yes, you do.* Be by yourself and try to be happy. Your work is cut out for you. How you balance your life is the key to your happiness and well-being. But your life can never be balanced if you do not have a daily practice.

Connecting. Do I have to explain to you what "connecting" means? Connecting to what? You know deep in your heart and soul what I am talking about. I am not going to patronize you. I am going to talk to you like the incredible, dynamic, resonant, vital being that you are. I want to speak to the wise one that lives inside of you, the compassionate one, the divine one, the hopeful one. When you read these words, which one of you is listening? I hope the many parts of you are listening to these words for the betterment of your life.

Do not spend your whole lives saying, "When I have the time I will do the thing that I love." When you make any advancement toward the thing that you love to do, the seas will part, and the stars will align, and all you have to do is love the thing you are doing with all your heart. Don't get distracted.

Know you can do and be even more than you think. Make the decision. Once you make the decision, it will all become easier. What is that decision? That decision is when you say to yourself: *I am going to do it, or I will die trying.* Your lives are worth it, you are worth it. Begin tonight. There's no better time than the present.

Chapter Six
The Mirror of Life

When you look in the mirror, what do you see? What are the feelings that go through you? Some of you spend very little time in front of the mirror. Some of you spend a lot of time in front of the mirror.

Maybe the ones who spend very little time in front of the mirror don't care about what they look like, or maybe they care very much and don't want to see because they don't like it very much. What about the ones who spend lots of time staring, analyzing, trying to fix? Maybe they care very much what they look like, or maybe they care too much what other's opinions are of what they look like. Maybe they are "fixing" themselves for others, but not for themselves. They are preoccupied with what others think of them. They are preoccupied with certain standards of beauty and your entire society is affected by this, particularly the young people and those who want to be young.

When was the last time you looked in the mirror and looked deeply into your own eyes? Can you gaze upon that person with compassion, to look upon that person as if it was the first time you have ever seen that person? What if you had decided to look into the mirror and pretend that you were looking at your long lost friend, or your long lost child, one you loved very much and whom you missed very much?

If you met a friend who you have not seen in a long time, a friend you loved and you were reunited with them, would it matter to you if their hair was messed up? Or their skin? Or if they were too skinny or too fat? Would you not just embrace them? You would be filled with the love you have held for so long. You would be so grateful that they were in your presence again. When you leave this life, you will not look back and say, "Who was the more beautiful to look at?"

I want you to look at yourselves in a new way the next time you look in the mirror. It is very interesting, when you go to purchase clothes you have three or four mirrors around you to see what you look like from every angle. Because of the placement of those mirrors you are able to see yourself from perspectives you are not used to, and this is where self-criticism becomes very strong. Because you didn't realize how you looked from the side, from the front, or from the top, you find many flaws within yourselves. You call them flaws. It is very rare you look at yourself and say, "Yeah, I look great."

You begin to make resolutions for yourselves that you will perhaps exercise more, or are more aware how you will wear your clothes, or how you are standing, so you feel you will look better. There is nothing wrong with that. It is good to have mirrors from every angle. Those are the mirrors for your physical selves.

What about the mirrors for the non-physical self? It is your environment, it is what is happening around you, and it is the people around you. They are reflections of what you are right now or they are reflections of what you used to be, what you want to be, or what you don't want to be, and of course, what you are. What occurs around you is a reflection of what is occurring inside you.

There are many people you meet that have a glow about them and you ask them, "What happened to you? Are you in love? Do you have a new partner? Wife? Husband? Girlfriend? Boyfriend? Did you get a new job?"

They say, "No, I changed my perspective, I am happier." But to you, perhaps it looks like they have lost weight or their skin is more glowing and probably it is, because they are happier. It is something inside that is shifting.

The same way that you use those physical mirrors when you are purchasing your clothes, and you see yourself from different angles, try to imagine mirrors for your mind and your emotions and your internal well being. Try to see yourself in those mirrors. They will tell you when you have too much anger, sorrow, ego, or sadness. What will be the exercises you do after you see those flaws? What will you then begin to do to begin to change those?

There are many things you can do. First, I will tell you what not to do. Do not condemn yourself for having those *flaws.* Do not beat yourself up anymore. Do not punish yourself. Many people punish themselves for overeating by starving themselves. That is not how you do it. You recognize you have overeaten and you begin to eat in a healthy, prosperous way.

Do not blame others. You have created your reality. Take responsibility. Here are some things you can do: Forgive yourself. Many times things that you consider to be flaws are simply reactions to protect yourself. To protect yourself from hurt, you become angry. To protect yourself from sadness you become distant. To protect yourself from fear, you become intimidating. You don't need to do any of those things. The Universe, the divine force that connects all things – you are one with it. It is one with you. It is always expanding. It is always aligning itself to become better. Yes, the Universe is becoming better. You may say, "But, I already think the Universe is perfect, nature is perfect." That is why it seems perfect to you, because it is always getting better.

When you look into the mirror and look into your own eyes, do this for several minutes: Try to understand the person who is looking back at you. Do not judge them. Do not praise yourself or blame yourself. Only try to understand and have compassion for who you are looking at. Imagine embracing this person, imagine comforting them. When you are embracing them, imagine holding their face and looking into their eyes and saying, "I believe in you." You have become disconnected from the many parts of you. What I mean to say, you have become disconnected from the love that you are.

You have been conditioned to things in your environment and because of your reactions to those things, to protect yourself, you have created layers and layers, shells over you. I am talking to the one who exists under all those layers, underneath all those shells. I am talking to the real you right now. Look upon yourself with love. Support and encourage yourself the way you would support and encourage your most beloved friend.

You would never insult or degrade or demean your friend. With this positive loving energy you direct toward yourself, you reconnect to the love that you are - the living, breathing, pulsating energy that you are.

When you look around you, it can seem everything is falling apart. Maybe you are losing your home, losing your partner, losing your friends, through death or misunderstandings, or losing your health. For many of you all of these things are happening right now, all at once. Some of you feel it is very cruel for this to happen to you, that it is the Universe that is doing this to you. Some of you feel it is a test for you to get some kind of reward. And for the rest of you, you feel it is by chance. *There is nothing by chance.*

The Universe is not making things happen to you or against you. There is universal energy. That universal energy can be tapped into. Many of you say, "That person is tapped in, or tuned in." That is given and taken as a compliment. That means that person has opened up inside to the flow of universal energy. They are "in the zone." When you are at a very tough point in your life, you tend to ask, "Why me?" It is because you have chosen this. I know this will be a hard one for you to accept but try to consider it, try to give it a chance, this theory.

I have spoken of the Higher Self. That is the version of you that is fully expanded and is its full glory, love, and power. You might say it is like the angelic version of you that is always hovering near, watching over you, saying to you, saying to your spirit, "Become one with me."

That Higher Self is always awake, helping to create situations and experiences that when properly integrated into your life, meaning you see them as growth experiences, and you can go through them with soulfulness, mindfulness, and compassion. Then you rise to a new level of being. You take your life to the next level.

You become closer and closer to becoming one with the Higher Self. All of your pain is simply your resistance in becoming one with your Higher Self. It is interesting, because you would think you would want to become one with your Higher Self, because the Higher Self sounds amazing and powerful – and it is! Who would not want to be the Higher Self?

You see, everybody wants to be their Higher Self. That is why they try to accomplish things all the time, mostly with their career. They try to get far, make money – it makes them feel more powerful. Or with love, they feel if they have a partner and they are in love, they have elation and joy, that they will feel and have what the Higher Self possesses all the time.

Even people who are abusing alcohol or drugs are trying to connect with the feeling of joy. But it is physically damaging and not long lasting. But the Higher Self exists without any of those things. You are not understanding the pain that you feel, the resistance to the growth experiences, the learning experiences that the *troubles* bring forward.

It is said in your society: *No pain, no gain.* But does that always have to be true? Don't you gain from feeling love? Don't you learn from humorous situations? As you grow spiritually, let me tell you, your sense of humor will have to expand! You will have to learn to laugh at your troubles and at yourself for getting yourself into those situations. If you were once wealthy and had many cars and now you are struggling to ride the bus, it is very difficult to find the humor in that. But once you do, probably your situation will change. If you stay stuck in the pain, in the fear, in the lack, then it feels like you are doomed.

In your world, you have to experience painful situations that will direct you toward the good situations. That is true in this dimension, but not so true in other dimensions. But that we will save for another book when I will tell you about the other dimensions. For now what I am telling you is when you feel painful situations, feel the pain but do not be stuck in it. If you ignore it, if you sweep it under the rug, it will not go away.

Sooner or later you will have to truly clean house. Do not wait for ten years from now when you are sitting in the psychiatrist chair or at the bar drinking, trying to drink your problems away, or in the arms of many people who do not love you and you do not love them. Make a loving commitment to yourself. Refrain from trying to love yourself by another person telling you they love you.

When you are in love, truly in love…what I mean is, inside the feeling of love, the vibration of love, the energy of love, you can flow more easily through your troubled times. Losing your house or loved one will be less painful and even your health will improve. Maybe you are thinking: *Oh, I have heard this before. Yeah sure, you have to love yourself before you can love anybody else. You have to love yourself if you want life to get better.* Perhaps you think that is cliché.

Do not concern yourself with if you have heard it before. Have you ever *listened* to it before? Have you ever *followed through* with it? Because no matter how many times you have heard it, if things are not going right in your life, it is because you are not feeling good enough during it, or to begin with, or things are not being maintained at a good satisfactory level. Maybe you did not feel deserving, so you lost things. Maybe you were always criticizing yourself, and so that created a negative energy around you and it destroyed certain relationships after a while. You can always trace it back to not always being very kind and encouraging to yourself.

When I talk about people around you that are mirrors, I am not saying listen to what they are telling you. I am saying try to listen to *who* they are and *what* they are. Are they kind or are they cruel, are they encouraging or discouraging? Do they stand for truth and love or are they negative? Who and what they are is reflective of your internal state. You may say, "I am losing my house, how does that reflect my internal state?" or "I have no job because there were cutbacks in my company and because of that I am losing my house, not my internal state." Let us go back to the Higher Self. Maybe it is the Higher Self who has arranged all this so you may become greater! Perhaps you can lighten your load along your journey. Perhaps it is for you to have less possessions or maybe to have a better house one day.

Maybe you are too attached to *this* house right now. You may love it, but maybe the Universe wants you to have something better. If you are a wealthy executive and you have lost your position in your company, maybe it is because the Universe wants you to spend more time with your family or friends or to see the world and not be so busy.

Maybe you have to move out of your wealthy neighborhood and go to a less wealthy neighborhood. Maybe that will take your mind off of the external, material things. In that time, the person who wants to get into that wealthy neighborhood, they buy that house that you were living in for a very cheap price, and now that person who was trying to attract better house for themselves gets to live in more affluent neighborhood.

They get to feel what it is like to have, in terms of material things, a better quality life. They get to experience something new, and the wealthy person gets to experience something new, both for their growth. The person who was poor now got to buy that better house in the better neighborhood. They have somehow manifested that from feeling deserving, and also the Universe worked with them for them to understand what it is like to live better. Same way the Universe is working with that person who was once a wealthy, very busy person, to reconnect with things they left behind or perhaps neglected.

It is not circumstance or chance. Everything is happening to make your experience better. What we mean by better? It is for you to become more and more your Higher Self and your Higher Self is truly who you are. Imagine opening the *Book of Life* in your hands. Imagine every page being a mirror. Look deeply.

Chapter Seven

What Is Your Truth?

You have been on a quest for the truth. You have read many books, sat in front of many masters, teachers, sacred environments, and you feel you are getting closer and closer to the truth. You are putting together pieces of truth that have been revealed to you or that you have discovered. How would you define "truth?" What is it? You are looking for something that you feel very strongly about. So when you say, "I want to know what the truth is…" The truth about what? Are you trying to define the word "truth" when you say that? Or are you asking for what the truth is about something in particular?

Does the truth change? There are scientific truths, are there not? If you combine certain elements, they will form water or gold. And you believe that this has always been true, and this will always be true. How can you say this will always be true? It has been true so far until one day it will no longer be true. You know, truth is always in the moment. Right now there are people marrying one another all over the planet. At this very moment that you are reading this people are saying, "I promise my life to you, to be the only one, the only partner for me, until death do us part." Is that true? They certainly mean it. Many of them mean it.

Right now it is true. If this marriage does not last and someday feelings have changed, the energy between the two people has changed, they may decide to end this marriage. Were they lying on the day of their marriage ceremony? The priest had said marriage is a sacred bond. Were they lying? The people who were watching the marriage ceremony were wishing well for the couple because of their belief in the purity of love and marriage. Were their feelings and good intentions also a lie?

Their intentions did not manifest in staying together. It is true then, their vows of love and commitment. But the energy, the spirit, the nature of that bond changed, and so it changed certain truths.

You may say, "But that is an emotional feeling, and the explanation about water and gold is scientific." I am telling you that one day perhaps it will not be true that certain combinations of elements will create something else. It can change, even in science. It is told to you by your scientists, that those other planets around you have no water so there cannot be any life. For them the truth is that water equals life. What if you were to meet beings from another planet that does not need water, only need some kind of mineral or dust or light from the sun to sustain life or to create life?

Look at all the stars in the sky. They are all suns with planets around them. There are infinite possibilities and infinite truths. Take a moment and try to define the word "truth." Maybe look it up in your dictionary. Don't you wonder what it will say? I am sure most of you have never bothered to look that word up in the dictionary. It is a very difficult word for you to define.

What about what some people call "eternal and universal truth?" There are a few, I must tell you. The number one is that "you create your reality." This teaching is spreading all over the planet, it is interesting. After you know that truth, why would you need to or want to hear another?

I want to talk about those of you that are always seeking the truth. When is it enough for you? When will it be enough for you? You are hearing these words now and perhaps tomorrow you maybe seek more from another teacher. Your bookstores are filled with books about the universe, truth, philosophy, metaphysical subjects. I can tell you, there are a certain small number of truths that those books are trying to say in their own way. It is like music; only certain number of notes but so many songs. You have not even heard all the combinations of those songs yet because there are songs being written today that you have not even heard yet. What truth resonates with you? That is the truth that you will accept in that moment. Another truth that at that moment does not resonate with you, you will not accept.

Many of you have said, "I never believed it when I first heard it, but now after many years, I now understood it." So what you once rejected as once being false, you now accept it as truth.

Also the reverse can be said. Maybe what would be helpful is to say, "I am not a truth seeker, but I am a soul that joyfully connects with universal teachings." This will prevent you from saying one teacher is better than another. Some of your greatest lessons will come to you from the simplest sources. While your mind is fascinated by esoteric teachings, by what you consider to be enlightened masters, the moments that actually change your life are the most human moments, the most human experiences.

You want truth? Watch a baby being born. Try to help a mother bring it out of them. You will forget about all of the esoteric teachings at that moment and you will come into the heightened state of full vibrational aliveness, awareness. You want truth? Lose yourself in the blue of the sky, the endless, endless blue. Feel it.

To *know* the truth and to *seek* the truth, it is nothing compared to *feeling* the truth. Truth is the ultimate style. Let your style be truth. No matter what you do, whether it is a creative effort, or expression or simply your daily interaction with others - when truth is your style, it is your connection with your own unique vibration that is unlike any vibration in existence. Many of you call that "being yourself." But not many practice it.

Do not believe the saying that "truth hurts." Change that saying to "the truth nurtures." The truth nurtures growth, alignment, and expansion if you let it. Try to relax yourself in the most troubled emotional times and allow the truth in what is happening to expand your awareness to the possibilities of what you can become, of what you can achieve, of what you can change.

If you are upset that someone did not tell you the truth, that they deceived you on purpose to take advantage of you, of course this is very disturbing and can be painful and damages relationships. That person who did not tell you the truth, was *not being true to themselves first,* for they did not trust or feel their truth was good enough to manifest positive outcomes in their lives.

So they had to change or disguise the truth in order for themselves to feel better. And you as a victim to that lack of truth, are being offered an experience to raise your appreciation of the teaching that to be true to oneself is beautiful and important.

Release yourself from this feeling of betrayal from that person not telling you the truth. You are adding more fuel to that fire. Have faith that the situation will not damage you. Understand the situation occurred to raise your understanding to a new level.

In your courts of law, they want to make people tell the truth so they say place your hand on a holy book. Because they feel that a person's oath to tell the truth is heightened by placing their hand on a collection of truths that they believed as a society to be eternal. They are starting from the assumption that the person who is about to be questioned will not tell the truth and will be tempted to lie.

So they make them swear, and yet many people still lie. Why? Because they do not believe what is in that book they are swearing on is true, or maybe they do not believe that taking an oath means something, so they lie. In the eyes of the world they have gotten away with it.

Maybe for that person, they feel no guilt, and maybe it takes time for the truth to catch up to them. Either way it is not something that you have to become preoccupied with. When you stand in your own truth…that is what is relevant. Keep in mind that your truth can change and will change. Be more flexible. Allow others to change their truth.

It seems to anger many of you when a person changes their allegiance. Why does it bother you so much? You are all on a truth seeking journey whether you realize it or not. Everything you do, you are trying to feel the heart of things. The heart of everything is its truth. Very simple.

When you say, "What is at the heart of this matter?" When you say "What is in your heart?" what you really mean is: *What is the truth?* Once you know what is in your heart - what that truth is - whether it is a bad feeling or a good feeling, when you know it and look at it and then you can accomplish things and align yourself to live a clearer and more productive life and develop a better communication with others.

Chapter Eight
Inner Vision

Your inner vision is the greatest gift that you have. Your inner vision is a power that if you tap into it, there is nothing that you cannot be or achieve. You were born with this inner vision when you were a child. It was easier to utilize it then. In fact all of your waking hours as a child were spent being one with your inner vision.

What do I mean? What even is "inner vision?" Let us start there. Your inner vision is the natural, flowing energy of projecting into physical reality that which you desire to feel. Your inner vision reflects what you really want from your experience in this life. Your entire life is one big process of allowing your inner vision to become reality – your dreams, your wish for emotional fulfillment.

Your inner vision, however, is something you take for granted. Isn't that interesting? You start to say that your inner visions don't really matter – that there is a reality that conflicts with your inner visions, your dreams, that it is not possible to always make your inner visions reality, for there are circumstances beyond your control that prevent it.

When you are an infant that inner vision is to walk, but your physical body – that reality – is that you can only crawl. So how did you learn to walk? The reality was your bones were not strong enough to walk. Your toes did not possess the power of balance. Your head perhaps was too big for your body, too heavy. Your spine did not have the stability, but your inner vision – oh, that had balance and stability and drive. It surpassed physical limitation, or what you would call reality.

Your mind, it is very interesting. Your mind that possessed these inner visions of communication and wanting to speak, was hearing the sounds of animals, the people communicating using language that you did not understand. But you went by feeling. You went by the vibration that you felt from the words that your parents were saying to one another, that your family members were saying to one another. Because you were pure awareness and sensitivity as a child and although you understood everything through feeling, you knew there were greater ways to communicate – by learning the language, by learning to speak. So there was an inner vision in this little mind that you could learn to speak.

There was such a powerful inner vision within the mind of this infant, that it could observe that there was a better way to communicate even though the tongue could not take the shapes to form the words, even though the brain did not know the words – again, your inner vision versus *reality.*

Over and over again, you began to prove, even as an infant that your inner vision could become reality. It is said amongst your people: *When there is a will, there is a way.* It is so true. But as you begin to get older, your mind and your brain begin to see a different reality. It started to agree with the physical reality. It started to see obstacles.

It started to see that you had to work around them, through them, get over them, and get under them. Your dreams, they go in the back seat and your mind begins to drive. You took your greatest gift and put it in the back seat. Those on your planet who you respect and you admire, they do not let their dreams be in the back seat. Their inner visions drive them through their lives at great speed, and in their actions they trust their inner vision.

I want you to think about what you had dreamed your life to be. What you had imagined it could be like - all of it. What kind of city did you want to live in? What kind of clothes you wanted to wear? What kind of name you wanted to have? What kind of person you wanted to be in love with? What kind of person you wanted to be in love with you? How much money you wanted to make?

The list goes on and on. Those are your inner visions. How many of them are true now? How many of them became real? What stopped you? What began to blind the inner vision? Doubt? Fear?

Well, I say to you do not trust your doubts. Doubt your doubts. Many of you think that it is too late, that you are too old, maybe too tired, not good enough anymore, or that you do not have the resources to reconnect to the dreams you once had. I am here to tell you that is not true.

You may spend your whole life in your mind, believing that there are no spirits, there are no angelic forces. I don't care who you are, you have experienced this kind of assistance in your life. Every person has had a moment that they said to themselves: *I cannot explain it but the help appeared out of nowhere.*

Maybe the time has come on your planet that you start to believe again in these things. The ancient people, they knew this and they accomplished much. Do you think that my people were not a wise people? Across the planet we have been known for our wisdom. My people believe in spirits, spirit guides.

You are being assisted. You are not alone. Today, you call it "positive thinking." If it helps you, then I am happy, but there seems to be a lack of love in that positive thinking. Where is the togetherness? Where is the co-creation? It does not matter what your religious beliefs are in this discussion.

You are aware of something - you are aware that you exist, and you are aware of that power through your life with the fuel of your emotions. Those emotions mean something. They are valid. You can move mountains with those emotions. You can do anything when you tap into the power of your happiness.

There are people on the planet that tap into the power of their anger and their own destruction – and they accomplish a lot in that destruction, let me tell you. In the name of God and religions they conquer other countries. There are always reasons to justify when that should happen, why it was good. There are always reasons. And then there are the people who work with their happiness, who build. They create, they co-create, they work with others, and they respect other people's traditions and cultures.

They are the happy ones. They are the ones who feel joy in their hearts and share it with others through their deeds, through their words, through their pure emotions that they are radiating in. You can be one of those people.

You were once one of those people when you were born. You were a person, when you were a child, who cared about the animals. When you were a child, you could not bear to see an animal get hurt, you defended those who were weak when you were a child. You touch the flower and you felt wonder, awe, inspiration. You were electrified. You saw a tree and you wanted to be in its arms.

The wind touched your face and you were delighted and exhilarated. The night would fall and you would feel one with the stars and the galaxies. You felt fully alive at all times. To sleep was not a challenge; it was easy. To smile at strangers was easy. To laugh just because somebody else was laughing was easy. Where did it go?

When you were sad, you began to feel self pity in your life. Your vision becomes clouded, your vision not so good. You do things perhaps you regret. You get blinded, blindsided, and many lessons are offered to you through experience and through people in your life, to regain your sight to help you see clearly again. If you are lucky, you get back on track. You begin to connect again, once again with your inner vision.

We want you to begin to see the change in your life actually appearing. My friends, see everything that you desire being real. Feel it in your bones, touch it, taste it, hear it, feel it. There is another aspect of your inner visions that have nothing to do with material success, but has to do with insights into people.

The first person to have insight into is yourself. How much time do you spend every day looking into yourself? I am not talking about, you know, what you want or what you want to do; taking care of yourself, the day-to-day matters. I am talking about spending time looking into yourself, asking yourself why you do the things that you do. If many people are telling you the same thing about you, don't you think it is wise to consider it? If inside you it is not true what they are saying, ask yourself: *Why do they think that which they say?*

You are living this life to improve, and as time goes on to get better in every aspect of your life. It is worth it to spend a few minutes a day to look inside of yourself and to see where you started certain patterns in your life. Look at the patterns in your life. Do not beat yourself up over them trying to figure it out.

It is like riding a bike. If you are leaning too far over to the left and you keep falling over, you are not going to yell at yourself; you only begin to lean the bike toward the right to center yourself. If you do feel that you are being very difficult on yourself, ask yourself: *Where did I learn that? Who did that to me? Was it my parents, teachers, siblings?* Many of you are too hard on yourselves. You do not believe in yourself anymore.

What do you do when you do not believe in yourself? What do you do when you truly believe whatever inner visions that you had, were a waste? Because many things in your life did not turn out the way you wanted, and many people whom you trusted and believed in and loved did not live up to what you had thought. Then what do you do? Then what good are your inner visions, your insights? What I am telling you is to never give up that which is inside of you, because it comes from an innocent place, a pure place.

The things that you find challenging and painful in your life are not there to distract you from your inner vision but to redirect you toward it. So now you know what you don't want, at least you are clear what you do want.

You have read many inspiring stories about many people overcoming incredibly difficult odds and challenges in their lives that go on to do extraordinary, powerful things. Never forget these stories. Remind yourself of them. Help yourself along in your day - maybe take their picture and put it on your wall. Maybe take many pictures of them! Maybe take their quotes and write them in a notebook.

These are practical things I am telling you. Are you embarrassed to do them? Why? Because maybe it will mean that you need help? You seek help - that is why you are reading this book.

So let us stop the pretense and the games right now. You need help. I want you to keep a journal. I want you to begin to write positive things about you. You might feel like you are lying at first, but I say don't trust that part of you. Keep writing.

Write what is good in your life. Write about the good things that your friends have done for you. Write about the qualities that they have, whether it is their laughter, their jokes, and their strength - whatever.

You may think: *Oh, yeah. I can do that.* But can you do it every day? Can you try to do it for a month? Maybe you will feel it is a waste after a few days. You may say, "Oh, what good is it to write those things? - they are not real." Then, oh, my friend, I have proven it to you. You don't believe. You are stuck in some kind of negative hypnotic state that you keep returning to.

You can break free of that. You can snap out of it. Do not let the negativity ruin your life. In your journal write down quotes of people who have said inspiring things. You may think to yourself: *I don't even know any.* You can find them. You can go on your computer and punch in "inspiring quotes" and you will find many. Oh, maybe you don't have the time, *huh?*

You don't have the time to do something that perhaps you think is silly. Maybe you have grown up too much? Maybe you have become so serious that if you have to do something that seems so silly, also seems like a waste of time. Children do not feel that it is a waste of time to do something silly. They think that is time well spent. And let me tell you, they are laughing a lot more than you.

They do not stay depressed like you do. They can be crying one minute and they can shift and be laughing the next. You see that perhaps as a weakness. We see it as strength, flexibility, spontaneity – constantly returning to the "inner vision" of happiness or well-being. Your natural state of existence is happiness and well-being. Your natural state of being alive is peace, love, and truth.

When you return to the magic of your inner vision, you will see reality match your dreams.

Chapter Nine

Abundance

Lately everybody has been talking about the word "abundance." In the old days, abundance meant there was a good harvest. Imagine a very large basket that was bursting with colorful fruit. Many fish in the net was "abundant." That which would feed us for the coming times was considered to be abundance. To feel the love of the tribe, the togetherness, the celebration of the many seasons - that was abundance. We were one with that process of abundance whether were fishing or planting, dancing, expressing love and joy - it was all about abundance. Now in modern times "abundance" has taken a different meaning.

Mostly it means having lots of money. I am not here to criticize the concept of money. We spirit guides understand it is the progression of society. It is no problem. Money is another way to understand abundance and on a particular level that is relevant to your current society. So let us talk about it. Because I know most of you don't want to talk about fruit and fish and dancing around the fire!

Some people will say that "abundance" is when more than your needs are met. What if your needs are different? What if your *need* is to have a very, very big house? Or have many cars? Many clothes?

Many fancy jewelry to wear? Material things can bring you delight... perhaps not eternal happiness, but certainly delight. How do you get more of these things that you desire of this world? How do you learn to receive them?

You have to learn how to receive abundance. How do you learn to receive something perhaps you have never had? Many of you who are reading this do not have the kind of money that you want to have. And you keep trying, and you keep trying, and you don't get it. How can you get something into your life that you don't even know what it feels like? You don't know how to receive it, for you have never received it.

If you have never received it, then how can you know *how* to receive it? You can receive love better than you can receive money, because at least somewhere when you were a baby you have received love even on some level. So it is easier to receive love than money, or so it seems. Maybe it is equal. It is not about receiving love or money – just to learn how to receive, period.

To be open to receive – how do you do it? Let us say you say, "Okay Red Eagle, maybe the Universe has many gifts for me like you say and all I have to do is open my arms. I have been opening my arms for more and more and more, but I am not receiving. How do you tap into that feeling if you have never had it?"

The *illusion* is you have never had it. Here we must go back to the simple things in life like your breathing, your heart beating, and your experiences of beautiful things that you have seen and touch and tasted, the moments of joy and wonderment you have experienced as a child until whatever age you are now. You may feel that those moments were few and far between, but does not matter. Many great lives have been inspired by one moment. One moment! You can do the same. Begin to see it in your life. Begin to reflect it in your life. Look at the things that have brought you great happiness, even if it is only for a short time. Do not say to yourself: *Oh, I had money then I lost it. Oh, I have felt love, but then I lost it.* I want you to concentrate on the *feeling* of having it. That is the key.

Are you open to receiving surprises? Gifts from sources you have not predicted? I am here to tell you that is worth waiting for, worth living for. Every day to see what gifts the Universe has in store for you, you have to feel deserving of those gifts. How much do you *feel you deserve?*

If I were to give you a blank check every day, how much would you write for yourself? When would it be too much for you? Every day, imagine, every day, maybe for a month, for six months, for a year, for ten years – would you get tired of writing yourself a check for a million dollars for ten years? How about a check for unlimited love, unlimited fun every single day for the rest of your life? How much guilt would you be building up inside of you? Ask yourself. Imagine it. You don't get what you deserve in this life. You get what you feel you deserve.

Think about the joy of giving. Think about the time that you have given something to someone and the joy in your heart. Imagine them rejecting it. In some cultures it is polite to say no to the gift. First they protest, "No, I do not deserve. You shouldn't have done that." It is a polite custom, they feel, and then they accept. It is not a rejection.

Haven't you been in relationships and the person had given love, and you have not been able to receive it? Or you have given them love and they have not been able to receive it? It is sad. You have many gifts in this lifetime. We feel it is not a question of deserving. It is a question of enjoying the giving.

Do you know giving can be a very selfish thing? And receiving can be a very selfless thing? It can be the opposite. Some people keep giving because they don't know how to receive. To receive gifts with open arms and no guilt is wonderful; to know it is more than about deserving. Gifts are the natural flow of universal energy and law.

Do you know in some cultures when a person saves another person's life, the person that saves them thanks them? If you save someone's life, never let them thank you. You should be thanking them for the experience. Perhaps you saved your own life - your emotional life - on this spiritual journey.

It is worse to live an emotionally oppressed life than to physically die. At least when you die, there will be some release. But when you live an emotionally oppressed life you are never free and you stay in poverty consciousness. Have you ever noticed that people that are poor say when they are poor, "If I get money, I promise to do this, I promise to do that, I promise to do these good things?" Those who are poor are very angry with those that are rich and they say, "If I had that money I would be helping that person and this person, I would do being doing this, and why is that rich person not doing that?"

You justify to yourself: *Oh, God will not be pleased with that.* You have created what we like to call your story, your version of events. Always *three* sides to a story - your side, their side and the truth... the facts. It is like a game of tennis. Let us say you did not know anything about the game. The facts are there is one person on one side of the net and another person on the other side of the net, and they are hitting the ball with a racquet. The ball went past one person and some people watching became happy and some people watching became sad. Those are the facts.

What you have created in that game is somebody won and somebody lost. "If you lose, you should feel bad." That is what you say to your people, to your children, to everyone. You lose the game, you should feel bad. You should have made the ball go past the other person and then you could feel good. It is a game, more so than you know!

Try to look at situations detached. Try to step back from them to see what is happening. Be flexible. Be changeable. You don't like to be on the side that is losing - you feel bad. Then why don't you switch sides? If your enjoyment is only about winning, then just switch teams. If it is about something more than that, then focus on the game as an opportunity to become better for yourself, not to make another person lose.

The people who are in the poverty consciousness have a lot of judgments. Did you know that? There are many cases of people who thought they would be different when they finally got a lot of money, but they are stuck in their mindset. They are not happy.

Those who have money, who get money much more easily, have flexibility. They see it coming in from here, there, and anywhere and they know more will come. You may say, "Red Eagle, are you saying that those who are stricken with poverty in the poorest countries of the world have to just think different, and their situation will change? They are no longer going to be peasants, corruption will disappear, and they will no longer be living with only seeds and grains barely enough to feed their families?"

I am not talking about those people. I am talking to the people reading this book. I am talking about the people who can make a difference to those other people in the world. Do not think your smart comments can keep you from understanding the truth about abundance, so get off of your high horse. When you learn about abundance and learn to receive in your life, you can do something to help your fellow man. When I am talking about being more flexible, I am talking about you.

Do not try to deflect by saying, "What about this poor nation and what about that in other parts of the world?" I am talking about *you,* your world, and your mind. I want to get inside of *you* right now so you can be free of this. I want to help you learn to master receiving so that you may give with an open heart and mind and teach others how to receive and give.

And it goes on and on and on. These ripples will reach to all parts of the world. It starts right now with you at this moment. But you are not seeing beyond having a little bit more money to have the car or house you want. You are not seeing beyond that. All of those who are reading this book can make a difference in the world. But your thinking is small right now. This is a time to think big about hope, love, and abundance. Share the harvest that you have cultivated through the seasons of your life.

How do you manifest? That is another word that you hear a lot about - "manifesting." Somehow the desire you have for certain things begins to generate energy psychically. How do you do it? You don't have to leave the chair you are sitting in right now to do it. You don't have to work harder. You only have to turn on the switch inside of you. What switch, is that? If you have to ask my friend, you will perhaps never know.

I want you to turn it on. Lift the switch! It allows the flow of energy to move through you.

Think of a lamp. It is plugged into the wall is it not? It is plugged into the power source. The bulb is inside the lamp but there is no light until you turn on the switch, it lights up. But if the light is not connected to a power source, it does not matter how many times you turn on the switch. We need to look at the spiritual side of this! Love is your power source. Love, faith, inner visions, is your power source. Your dreams are your power source. Your demand for a great life is your power source.

Even your disgust at a disappointing life is a power source. Strength for those that are weak and oppressed across the planet is your power source. Plug into *that*. Then turn on the switch. You will see a difference. Start to observe the blessings right now. You can begin by starting to read a book that can be of use to you. You can start where you are sitting or standing right now.

Perhaps you can start wearing an article of clothing that looks very nice on you. Can you feel it? Can you enjoy it? Can you be grateful for it? The structure that you are standing or sitting in is not falling apart. There is something to look forward to later, whether it is a meal or a conversation with a friend, or a restful sleep, or a nice warm bath or shower. There is always something to be thankful for.

Even if you cannot look forward toward anything later on today, you can look forward to reflecting on good memories. Your good memories are also a strong power source. The feeling of quenching your thirst can be a power source. Do not feel that which you desire is far away from you. There are ways to bring them closer.

People create something called vision boards. Do you know what that is? You take a big piece of kind of cardboard and put many pictures - cut up pictures from magazines, newspapers or something, book of things you desire - and you put them on the vision board. You paste them. It is a simple exercise. Perhaps you have heard of it. Red Eagle has not created it, but I am talking about this basic exercise.

Those of you that have done it before, maybe do it again if you have some time, and make a newer vision board. To those of you who have never done this exercise before, it can be fun. When you were a child you used to have fun doing things by yourself. Why don't you try doing it again to get out of your routine, my friend?

Go back to the basics. Find pictures of a happy couple together you see walking on the beach, or maybe a nice stereo, a nice television. It can be material things, spiritual things, simple things, it can be cars. Put it on the vision board and fill it up. Don't just put one thing, put many, many things. It could be the body you wished you had. Put it in front of you somewhere you can see it every day and know it will be real.

Here is another game you can play. If there is something simple, like a car that you wish to have, you should go to the car dealer and sit inside it. You may not be able to afford it right now, but when you touch it, when you sit inside it, when you feel it, your body will feel good and say: *Yeah, it feels good, I belong here.* Take it for a test drive and have fun. Do not say, "I cannot afford this, why am I playing this game?" I am telling you very directly you need to start playing games.

Don't get uptight thinking about this. I am telling you need to be loose and start having fun to manifest things in your life, not to be so serious all the time. I know it is a wild concept for some of you out there, because you have learn to work hard, harder, and hardest, then you will get some of what you want, but you will not get all of what you want. But you will get some things that will satisfy you enough. Why it cannot be a concept for you to enjoy everything you do?

Can you work pretty hard, not too hard, and enjoy it and get double of what you earn? What about triple? What about you get ten times what you earned? You see, the word "earning" is very tricky. It is a deception. When you love someone, did they earn your love or you just love them?

You say to yourself: *I don't know why, I just love that person.* It is instant connection, no rhyme, no reason, and it does not matter. Your feeling is your feeling. They did not earn it; it is not even a question! It is only because they are completely recognized by you, isn't it? They don't have to do anything to earn your love.

Believe it or not, that is how the Universe works with you. Why do you think there are so many people who are very famous and they make a lot of money, who you feel don't have any talent? You cannot understand why so many people like their face, music, or their movies, or their books, or their words – it does not matter. You don't understand it, you will never buy it.

But those people who have created it have the abundance that you want. It is not about what *you* feel they deserve, it is about what *they* feel they deserve. The sooner you get that my friend, the sooner your abundance will come and your judgments will be gone. And you will then learn you don't have to have judgments and strict belief systems. See it for what it is – the flow of energy. If you remember, you can go against the flow or go with it.

You are pure abundance already. Do you know your body right now is manufacturing cells? Recreating and duplicating them? When you feel good, you look better. When you feel bad, you look worse. Very simple math. Your emotions affect your reality. What proof do you need?

It is always easy to tell when somebody is in love. They are glowing. It is always easy to tell when someone is feeling bad. They are walking down the street, their shoulders are humped over, their chest is caved in, the eyes are dropped, head is hanging down, and their body starts get that way, and they feel old and debilitated.

When you feel happy over the years, abundant and have vitality, you will have continued abundance. When you realize that *you yourself are abundance,* everything that you desire seems very easy to achieve. Keep working on this, friend. I don't expect you to get it overnight, but perhaps you will begin to see the path lighting up. I believe you can do anything you want to, any time you want to because nature is abundant. You are a part of nature and the harvest will begin and never stop, my friend.

Chapter Ten
Self-Mastery

Sometimes you will say, "I will believe it when I see it." You need to see it with your own eyes and then you will be convinced that it is true. It is something you live by, maybe it is not enough to smell it or hear it. Maybe it is not even enough to feel it – but you say, "I will believe it when I see it."

Maybe you have heard of things that seem unbelievable, like right now the fact there is a spirit speaking, dictating this book – maybe that is unbelievable to you. You are holding it in your hands and you are reading these words. You are seeing it. Maybe if you follow the advice of Red Eagle you will see changes in your life and you will believe it.

You will see changes in your life and then you will believe it. Or perhaps something of this metaphysical or "supernatural" thing is something you can put aside, something you don't want to deal with even though you see it and you see it is working, so you must believe it.

You see, your body – let us start with the first thing. If I were to tell you all the incredible mechanisms and processes and self-correcting measures that your body takes, you seem to accept it, but really how do you believe it?

If we were to take out your liver from your body and put it on the table, it is only a piece of meat - you can cut it open and all you will see is meat. It is laying there lifeless, deaf, dumb, and blind...or so you think.

You can say the same thing for your kidneys, your spleen - a tiny little thing, only it is shaped differently but it is made of the same thing as the liver - flesh and meat, slimly, slippery. But when you put it in your body, you put it into context, and that piece of meat that you call your liver knows what to do. It knows that its function is very different than what is the function of the kidneys or spleen. You can put something into your body and the liver knows what to do. It can identify if what you put into your body can be used or not.

Every organ in your body also knows the cells and the subatomic particles in your body. The liver can speak to the kidneys, to the spleen, to the stomach. It can speak to the heart, who can speak to the brain. Everything is communicating. But it does nothing when it is not in the body.

Your brain is only a piece of flesh, look at it, and imagine it right now. You accept that knowledge is stored in there, stored where? In the flesh? Remembering the lesson you learned, the code for your bank machine, somebody's name is stored in there. But if you were to slice the brain open you cannot find it. You only know through your fancy machinery what part of the brain lights up when you think about certain things, and what parts does not. You also know that most of your brain you don't even use. Or perhaps you think you don't use it, or perhaps the machinery that you are used to testing whether you use both of your brain or not can't even do the job.

Think about it. You had telescopes hundred years ago. They could not see the things you see now with the newer telescopes. Does that mean that those galaxies were not there a hundred years ago, because you could not see them because your telescopes were not powerful enough? Simple.

A hundred years ago, I am sure there were some scientists who believe there are other galaxies you could not see, and there were other scientist who said, "We cannot see anything out there, so they are probably not there." Those scientists that have faith for what they could not see, but believe they must be there, were proven right.

Those that went by what you call the facts, were proven wrong. This can be applied to any part of your life. Maybe you don't have the tools to see something about your life right now, something that is true. Maybe it is something that is a very positive thing – that you are good enough, smart enough, hard working enough, lucky enough, good looking enough – you cannot see that.

Maybe you are being too selfish, too unkind, too inflexible, too sad, too fearful, but because right now you don't have the tools to see it, you just wonder what is wrong and why you are not getting what you want out of life. This is logic my friends. This is not some kind of vague idea.

What about: *I will believe it when I hear it?* Some people say, "When that person tells me what they feel, then I will believe it. But they have to tell me they are upset, they have to tell me they are happy, and then I will believe it." Maybe there are things that you cannot hear because you don't have the ears for them. Look at dogs – that whistle that is special for dogs. If you blow it, only the dog will hear it. If you blow it, you cannot hear it. You might as well throw the whistle away unless there is a dog that can hear it.

Do you know there are colors that exist that you don't even know about? I am not talking about shades of green and blue or green or yellow and different variations. I am talking about completely different colors. You cannot imagine that. It would blow your mind trying to imagine that. *What do you mean there are colors that I have never seen that don't even look like any other colors that I know?* I am telling you there are. Your perception can only see the various shade of the rainbow. From red to violet – that is the spectrum.

What about smell? There are some people who can smell smoke, who get into a car and smell something funny and say, "I should not drive this car today," or walk into a building and smell something strange and know there is a gas leak. You can't see it, but it doesn't mean it is not there.

What about: *I will believe it when I _feel_ it?* You will also feel it when you believe it – that is a better way to look at it. You walk through your life saying, "When I feel it I will believe it." First you think you need to feel it to know it. That seems very logical to you. And on the surface it seems logical, I agree. But if you have never had something sweet, how can you believe something sweet exists, or sour, or bitter, or salty, without experiencing it?

When you were born, you felt love; you didn't get born believe in love or hoping to have love. You were born *into love.* Does it make sense that you were born into anything else but love? Somewhere in your heart of hearts you believe love is the greatest power. A baby does not say, "When I feel love I will believe it." They are already feeling it! It is natural to believe it. It is reality. That baby was you. Somewhere along the line you got disconnected to this reality. You got disconnected to this connection, to knowing that everything in its base is love.

So when you say: *I will believe it when I _see_ it,* what about your religions? Did you see all of those prophets? Did you see the parting of the seas? Did you see any of the miracles in whatever religions you have followed or you have grown up around? They are stories, are they not? I am not saying they are not true or not saying that they are true. I am saying you have read about them in a book. That is a fact. You know those religions because you read about it in a book and because everybody you knew were talking about this book.

That is a fact. You cannot argue with it, you have no chance to argue with this fact. So you read about these things in a book, and were told about these things in a book from a young age. Everyone you saw who was experiencing something good in their lives was attributing it to this book. When things were going wrong, they found solace in this book. So what you began to see was other people's reactions to their belief systems and then you believe it too.

You see, when you were young and full of love, those people who were giving you love - whatever they say starts to become law. How they act toward each other, what they believe is good in the world or bad in the world, you were recording it, recording it, recording it. You were innocent to it. You were like a sponge.

The amazing thing is that even while you were recording it, absorbing all of these things, there is a part of you that has its own mind and your own belief system. You pushed it aside. You will not remember because it was so long ago, and that decision changed the entire course of your life - it is so deep within you.

Somewhere in your growing years you thought that you needed proof. You were taught this. You needed proof to show that something is real. But what is proof really? The scientists will say there is no proof God exists and the people who believe will say God exists. *We have this book and that is proof enough for us. We see the flowers, the trees, the oceans and that is proof enough for us. The animals are proof enough for us.*

The scientist say, "We have studied the minerals and the various explosions that have happened in the galaxies, and the cosmic dust and gasses and all the fluctuations, everything we have seen prove how life has happened." So they will forever be at odds. Now they are saying, the scientists are saying, "We have created God. There's a reason for things, maybe there is an energy that connects everything, there seems to be." Maybe that is what people are talking about, and the people who believe in God are saying that God created the scientist. So we have somebody to argue with or to save. That is a big one for people isn't it? - having to save everyone else.

You are all here for your own journeys. You should be busy trying to save your own self. And by saving your own self you can save the world. Because ultimately by saving your own self, you will begin to love yourself and you will begin to love others.

You got indoctrinated into a system of thinking, which was: *Show me proof.* You need proof of its value also. It is simple. Money is only a piece of paper, but everybody agrees that it is worth something. You give somebody that piece of paper with a number on it, and they will give you something that they believe that is worth equal value of that piece of paper. So your whole world runs on this system. How much something costs, what is the benefit, or what is the potential damage? That is how everything works. In going into love relationship or business relationship, you say, "What is the good that can come out of it? What is the worst that can come out of it?"

When it comes to the idea of needing things to be proven to you, remember something. Many theories that were proven to be true for so long, later were proven to be untrue.

So what ultimately can be proven? What if you decided you don't need proof anymore, that what you *feel* is proof enough? Maybe there is a lot of room for arguments here. Maybe you say, "Red Eagle I believe that the sky is green." Okay.

And others will say to you, "No, it is blue."

Maybe the whole world will say, "No it is blue sky. If it is green prove it to us."

You will probably not be able to prove it, but you can go on feeling it is green if it makes you happy and it works for you. So be it. What you believe ends up what you see. If you believe there are happy people in the world, you will see them. If you believe there are beautiful miracles happening all of time, you will see them. If you believe that each day you are getting better, body, mind, and spirit.

Your scientists they are baffled, they give one person medicine and other person fake medicine and the one who gets fake medicine gets better, and they say, "Oh, placebo effect." That is all they have to say. They do not want to go into the power of the mind and the spirit system or the magic or belief.

Why is it always obvious when a person is in love? They have a glow about them. They look good and they feel good. Every one of you has appreciated the beauty found in simplicity. You can see something that is very ornate, very complicated in its beauty, and then somebody comes along and does something very simple, so honest, that you can feel it. Whether it is a work of art or even a meal, a simple home cooked meal compared to a very elegant, complicated, sophisticated gourmet meal, you go by the feeling.

Start to believe again. Start to believe in yourself again. Start to believe in life again, in love again. Start to believe in the goodness of others again. Never stop. No matter how many things or people you encounter that disappoint you, never betray your commitment to all that is good. You are good in your heart. In the deepest part of you, you are good. You can be good again. You can shed all the things that people have said about you that have held you down. You can shed all the skin that needs to be shed from you, that you and yourself can clear.

If there never was a mirror and you never got to see yourself anywhere, what would you think of yourself? Would you only think of other people's opinions of you? What do you see in the mirror? Is it someone who you can believe in? Is it someone who deserves another chance in life? Is it someone who deserves love? Success? Can you give it to that person that you see in the mirror? Can you believe in them? If you can, that means that you believe first and you can see it happening, all the good things. This will change your life forever.

One of the most difficult things for a person to do is change their mood. It is very hard to do. It takes a lot. Sometimes it takes a lot of things to happen, a lot of people to intervene when their friend is feeling very bad or very down. I am talking about the negative. It seems negative moods have so much power. You could be having a great day, and a bad thing happens to you and suddenly you say, "I was having such a great day and now my day is ruined." I understand it seems that way.

When you are angry about the situation where somebody do something you don't like, maybe a friend do something disrespectful to you, maybe a group of friends go somewhere together and they do not invite you. And when you find out, it is so painful for you, you feel betrayed and unwanted and unloved. You feel insulted. Maybe you feel people are sneaking behind your back. Maybe you feel they will talk negative things about you when they are together, how they enjoy life and how they don't want you there. Suddenly tension enters your mind with all these emotions swirling, most of them having to do with rejection. That is the root, obviously. You have been rejected.

How do you get out of that mood? What about if somebody at work, someone you do not get along with, you cannot stand their personality…everything they say eats away at your skin, they are very rude. They make your day ruined and when you get home you are agitated just thinking of that person. Or the person you are in the relationship with is not showing you love to you the way you desire.

Now that is creating moods, and I am giving you different moods as examples. Sometimes you wake up and you are in a lousy mood for no reason at all. That has happened you wake up and say, "This day does not feel right to me." Some of you try to cheer yourself up, you call a friend, maybe you go shopping, you eat something that will make you feel better, you do your exercise, maybe you make love, and maybe you have an argument. Yeah, people use arguments to feel better about themselves. Do you not know that?

I am talking about the ones who create arguments, who are looking for confrontation every day, and because when they have confrontations, they feel empowered. People take alcohol and drugs to change their moods. I will say one thing, I will give you credit for trying to change your mood. But look at this fact about human beings: They are always trying to feel better. You want to feel good. Everything you do or say or think in some way is in an effort to feel better. The fact that you are trying proves this, that it is in your nature to feel good.

When you don't feel good you feel out of balance, so that means that life is about feeling good. Simple. When you are in a bad mood, in your heart of hearts you know that it would be nice to feel good. But many people go further and further into their dark moods and they begin to mix all sorts of emotions in there – self-pity, that being the main emotion. Feeling bad for themselves – which means they want love, they want someone to help them feel better. So by going into self-pity you are trying to give yourself love but you get caught in the swirl of darkness, you know?

Turning upside down over and over like you are in some kind of washer machine that never ends and it does not feel good. As a matter of fact even your body will start to feel unhealthy. Your body gives many signs. You think too much, you get a headache. Your emotions are hurt, the middle of your chest gets very tight. You are not *saying*. You are crying, holding it in. You are not able to get the tears out, and your throat starts to hurt. You are disgusted with something, and your stomach wants to throw up. You don't feel supported, and your knees give out. If you can't hold onto something or someone, your hands are shaking because they are nervous. If a place feels strange and creepy, your skin begins to crawl. This is with everyone. There are no exceptions. You feel very alone, you feel cold. And you are under the heat of life, and you start to sweat. And it goes on and on.

What are some ways that we can change our moods? Well, I will tell you and I hope that you will consider it. Meditation is one of them. Some of you have been practicing meditation and some of you have never done it before. Start with the basics, learning to breathe again. Why is it, even doctors will tell you if you want the pain to be less when they stick you with a needle, to just breathe, breathe in and out, breathe deep, and they give you the shot and the pain goes away very quickly?

There is something very magical about learning to control your breath. Taking long, deep inhalations, holding your breath for a few minutes and to release long deep exhalations, it calms the body, the nerves, and the emotions.

You have read about it, you have seen it all over the world, on television, in magazines, on the radio, everywhere you have heard people are benefiting from meditation. Why don't you try it? Do you know, those of you that think you have not meditated, I will tell you that you have meditated. When you drive a car, I am sure you have noticed and experienced that you are driving along and suddenly you realized you have not been paying attention for the last ten minutes. And you wake up. I don't mean that you have fallen asleep. I mean that your consciousness was not there. You have woke up and realized you have not paid attention for the last ten minutes. Your mind was somewhere else.

Maybe you were not thinking of anything, maybe you were kind of zoning out. But you did not crash your car. You did not go too fast or too slow. You were on autopilot. That is one example of a kind of meditation. When you are focused on something - that is another type of meditation. When you are riding a bicycle, when you are reading something, or writing something, whatever you are doing, as long as you are intensely focused, that becomes a type of meditation.

When you do something long enough with an intense focus, you don't even know how many hours has passed. Suddenly time does not even mean anything; you have even changed your perception of time! You are not hungry; you even change the perception of your body.

So that is a kind of meditation, learning how to breathe properly again, it will change your life, my friends. You don't have to look far to learn how to do it. Just ask around, look for classes and look for books. Do what you would normally do when you are trying to learn about something.

Don't you want to learn about something that would benefit you? And those of you that already practicing meditation and are not doing it with all your heart, and not doing it regularly, yet you believe that meditation is something that can change the world - little bit every day will go a long way.

There are other ways that can change your mood: Listening to music, hearing it and letting the vibration to the music that you enjoy fill your ears, fill your mind, and fill your spirit. Music that you like carries vibrations, release things in your body, endorphins. Those are the body's natural pain killers. Calling a friend, a person whom you love and asking them to help you get out of the mood you are in.

People that are in bad moods, they never ask for help. It is like a person driving around, they are lost and they don't stop to ask for directions. They only keep driving, driving, driving…ending up frustrated, crying on the side of the road and out of gas too. Learn to ask for help sometimes. There are people who care.

"Self-mastery." That is a powerful term. It is not about how you learn to be the best athlete, or the best physician, or the best doctor, accountant, mechanic, cashier, sales person. That is not self-mastery. That is mastery of a particular field. Self-mastery truly has to do with something very simple: Can you control your moods? To control anything, you have to understand where it comes from. You have to understand its origins and its roots, asking, "What is the story of this thing?"

When two boxers are going to fight, do you know they watch videos of their opponent the past few years to see how they fight? *Oh, he punches like that, and then he moves like this.* They study it. They know when they get in the ring, they have to handle it, they have to survive, and they have to win.

Your moods, your emotions are like that opponent, but I actually do not want you to knock them out. I want you to make peace with them and see there is no reason to fight again. Tell your negative emotions, "Take off the gloves, I get the message."

So you have to learn to understand why your moods are appearing. Do you know oftentimes when you are arguing with someone, and you yourselves are telling them why you are angry, do you know that is not really what the problem is? Even though you believe that is the truth, you know your own truth and why you are angry. There are deeper and deeper and deeper truths. Usually one of the truths is that you are insecure and you will have to shed many layers to get to that level, because you have trained yourself to make yourselves right, to defend what you think is right about your opinion, and try to constantly try to make yourself feel better at every turn.

So I am going to ask you to do something that requires you to tap into your own power. I am asking you to do something that requires you to display your highest wisdom and your biggest heart, to be courageous. You know, the greatest battles are the battles within, my friend. Not the battles outside with other people, but the battles within yourself.

You need to get out of your own way. You have heard that one before. When you do get out of your own way, you are going to look back and realizing the "you" which was in your own way, wasn't really you to begin with. It was just a product of your own hypnotic self, self deprecating pattern. When you were a child, it was easy to change your mood – I mean when you were very small. You cry, somebody gives you taste of something sweet and you are happy… and your mood completely changed in one second.

You were a master for a little while of letting go of the mood you were in. You were a master of trusting again, starting anew again. I am not saying that you have to be that way for the rest of your life. I am saying you can tap into it a little bit. Just like sometimes you have fun, you tap into the kid in you, but you don't forget that you are an adult.

I am asking you to tap into some of the powers and flexibilities and to rediscover those parts of yourself. As you grow older, you begin to hold onto your mood longer and longer and longer, because your mind is getting more sophisticated, assessing more, and holding onto more, understanding many, many things in the world, more like why people do things, why they don't do things.

You get confused about those things as well and you need explanation. So the battle of the heart and the mind began, but nobody was teaching you wisdom. There is great peace and joy when you become one with your Higher Wisdom in you, when you start to letting that Higher Wisdom lead you through your life, lead you through your relationships.

The judge in you are the demons in you, that is the only demons that exist – the judge in you toward yourself and others. But mostly toward yourself because when you learn to forgive yourself, you can forgive others, and when you can forgive others, then you can also let them go. When you don't forgive them, they stay around energetically in your life. It is your anger, your negative emotions that will bind you to them, until you release them with forgiveness.

They will have to be set free from you, so you see I am not saying to forgive someone who is abusing you and continue to have interaction with them. I am not saying that by forgiveness you are saying that what they are doing is right or correct. I am saying it is how you process it for yourself, so you can become a master at it, so you truly can enact thought and actions toward yourself that are truly beneficial toward you.

Do you know by forgiving someone, you are releasing a lot of tension in you that is holding you back? When you are release them that way, then they become meaningless. They don't have any meaning in your life anymore and most of the time those people will continue to behave the way they behave because they have not truly tried to be masters of the self. And then you can go on to allow more goodness and joy into your own life.

Let's say you are in a situation with a group of people. You are all together and the group wants to go somewhere but you don't want to go there. So you are in a bad mood because you are being forced to go, and you are saying to yourself: *I will not have fun.*

Why would you say that to yourself? The only reason you are saying that to yourself is because you want to make yourself right. You want to prove to yourself that you knew they should not all go there for dinner. You are hoping something will happen subconsciously that will prove that it will be the wrong choice.

Then when everyone is having a bad time, ah, you are happy, satisfied in some strange way. What about being happy for others that they all agreed on something? What about remembering it is only one meal and you will have another tomorrow and another, and life is full of wonderful gifts for you that you will have whatever you want, and your turn will come? Do you know you can make your mood better by tapping into the happier moods of others? Happy moods can become contagious.

If everybody was learning to master themselves and put themselves in a better mood, do you know what kind of day you would have just going to the bank, or to the market, or driving your car, and pulling up to the red light and looking over and seeing somebody smiling at you hoping that you have a good day, nodding in the knowledge that both of you recognize that it is a beautiful day? Sounds like a pretty good world, eh? It can be and it is.

There will be people you will encounter that only want to stay in their bad moods, so let them. Smile and stay in your own vibration! Keep your vibration strong. You are committed to having a good day and don't say to yourself: *I am not going to let some jerk ruin my day.* Don't say that. Say, "There are people out there and they are in charge of their happiness." And when you do that, you know, you will no longer be insulted by what people do. It will only last a second. You will get insulted at first, and then you remember: *Oh it is because they don't know how to be happy.*

The secret for this to work is you have to learn how to be happy and then you will really believe it. So when you say it, you will know it to be true at the very core of your body.

Do whatever you can to change your bad mood! Your bad mood will not do you any good. The only time it will do you any good, is sooner or later you will get disgusted with it and you have to get angry, and anger gives you energy to change your situation. That can work, but to make a life of that can be exhausting, my friends. I am not condemning you for being in a bad mood. It happens.

These worlds is a very interesting and crazy school, but little by little try to practice what I am advising you, try to notice it more, don't beat yourself up over having a bad mood. Then you are ruining the whole idea of fixing your mood because now on top of it you are beating yourself up. Just remember the key to self-mastery is being able to tap into the ability, power, and magic to changing your mood. Change your mood and the world change, your life change, you change. You master your Self.

Chapter Eleven

Death

Of all the fears that the people around the world have in common, death is the strongest. There are some cultures, of course, on your planet that are not afraid of dying. They are mostly the tribal cultures, the ones where death is a part of life but not separate from it. These tribal cultures, those which are still around today, kept these traditions. Some of them even *celebrate* death. It is more like a bon voyage party wishing the person well as they cross into the other dimension.

Many of your religions, much of their influence on you, is based upon your fear of death and what happens to you after you physically die. Most of them will all agree your soul continues onward. But the reward is a physical Heaven and the punishment is a physical Hell.

Think about it. They will admit that the soul is not physical, but the punishment for the soul is physical. You will be rewarded in Heaven by many beautiful things to drink, and to see, and to feel, and to touch. And Hell you will feel the pain of fire and brimstone. So which one is it? Are you physical or non-physical?

We will talk about that later. But let us first talk about this idea of death. Some of you believe that death is simply a transformation; it is the next stage of rising, ascending, expanding as a soul, and that there are more journeys to take after in other dimensions if you also believe in reincarnation. Then there are other people that believe you live maybe seventy, eighty, ninety years and then you die. Based on what you did in those seventy, eighty, or ninety years you will be rewarded for unlimited time or punish you for unlimited time. Hey, what happened to: *The punishment fits the crime?* If you did eighty years of bad things, should you not get eighty years of Hell? Why an eternity of Hell? That does not seem very fair.

Or you do eighty years of good things and get rewarded with eternity of Heaven? I am not trying to make fun of anybody's religious beliefs. I am asking you to look at it with fresh eyes. There is no doubt of the beautiful creative force that surrounds us, that is within us, that I am talking about - it is your obsession with death, and your desperation toward life.

Even when you talk about master teachers and prophets like Jesus, it seems much of the world is more concerned with how he died than how he lived. It can be said about many of those teachers that walked the planet. Why don't you pay more attention with how they lived - without prejudice and with compassion - and have love for all human beings and creatures? Why don't you become obsessed with *that?* There have been as many female teachers as male teachers but they did not get the recognition. Now that is changing. There will be more balance in that area.

You spend your life trying to stay alive. It is instinctual. If a car is coming at you, your instinct is to jump out of the way. Even if you are suicidal, it takes a lot for you to stand in the way of that car. You are trying to avoid pain at every turn. It seems you are more concerned with avoiding immediate death, because that is much more clear to see the physical immediate death than the long term slow death.

What is "slow death?" Slow death is how you poison your body, it is how you poison your mind, and it is how you poison your heart. You poison your body with the improper foods and the unclean water you put into it. You poison your mind by listening to negative thoughts and information on the news and newspapers. You poison your heart with jealousy, regret, sorrow.

All of these things are a slow death. And that is something you don't seem to want to avoid, because it is slow and in little doses every day, it is tolerable. From our perspective, from the spirit guide perspective, we cannot understand how you tolerate it. But you are seeking ways to ease this kind of suffering. Some are very productive and peaceful, and enjoyable ways, beneficial ways, and some other ways like obsessive consumption of alcohol and drugs, add to your suffering.

If you can see the inside of your bodies or your hearts in some sort of physical way, you can see the dark matter, the dirt…I am talking about dirt in the sense of negative emotion that is trapped inside of you. If you can see it in some sort of picture, something like when people who smoke can see the blackness in their lungs in the x-ray, then it scares them, then they change their ways. If you can see how you have been holding negative energy in the physical body, you will do much change in the way you think and feel.

Why does it have to be that after a certain age you begin to deteriorate, why do you accept this? There have been many examples in your life where you see the principal of mind over matter. I shall say "spirit over matter."

Many of you have had relatives in your families that have done many bad things to their bodies, maybe smoke for many, many, years but still seem to be doing very good at an older age, or many people who work very hard and are still working hard into their seventies, and eighties, and nineties. What do they know that you don't know? Or what are they able to achieve within their spirit that you are struggling with?

Some of you are twenty-five and are feeling old already. Some are fifty-five and are feeling more energetic than a twenty-five year old. When you place your spirit into the arms of love, the slow death will no longer be. What does it means to "place your spirit into the arms of love?" You should be able to imagine it. It means that love carries you, that love carries you throughout your life.

Love for being alive. Love for appreciating the different types of people that are around you, the different cultures, the different animals, different art and music. It goes on and on, there is so much to see and to do in this world and many of you feel that you have seen it all and done it all. Many of you know that is not true. Some people do not believe that life is simply to experience all of it and to do all of it. Of course not. It is only to do and experience that which resonates with you, that you desire, your own preferences.

All of you - if you are to truly be free and tap into realizing that which you desire - it would be a very long list. There are people out there who have this list, that feel that they have to do everything on that list before they die. What happens then when you reach the end of the list? You die? What if while you were doing everything on the list there were more things created out there that you yet don't know about that would be very intriguing and inviting for you to experience? Then there can be a whole other list.

I will tell you something that some of you will find controversial: *You choose when you die.* Some people will be nodding your head as they read these words and some will be very offended and say, "What do you mean? Does that mean my little child chose to die in that accident or my mother chose to die very horribly in that disease?" First, let me start by saying that we know losing someone is very painful. But, as we are in spirit, we know something that you don't know.

Your child that died in that accident and your mother who died from that horrible disease are much bigger souls than you realize. This much bigger soul is living in other dimensions still connected to the higher dimensions, and the smaller version of that soul that is living on planet Earth is not so aware of the larger soul, the larger part of the soul that is living in the other dimensions. We call that the "Higher Self." The Higher Self is guiding, and when it feels that its lessons have been learned on this planet and there is nothing more here for them to learn, then they leave.

Even in episodes of traumatic experiences, even through disease, many of these souls who come for a short time to the planet are here to teach us. Many of them are teachers. What are they here to teach us? Depends on the person, but collectively I will say for us simply to love them and appreciate the time they spent with us, to look at what they suffered through in their life - whether it was a troubled soul or a very happy soul - to look at their experiences and to learn. Perhaps my explanation will only make sense to you if you accept that this life, this planet, is a school. Then it will make sense to you. Look at your life and everything in it as a school and everyone on your planet are your classmates.

You have teachers and you have classmates, some who are more advanced than you and some who are not as advanced as you. You share information with each other. You look to the teachers and ultimately you become the teacher.

You are always asking the universe, why this certain particular person die when they were so good? Do you think that is a punishment? I can assure you that person who has crossed over is not feeling any pain. Again, this is a matter of your belief, but I have come to give you this kind of message and you can take it or leave it. You can take the time to consider it, and if it makes you feel better, then you can believe what I am saying. Then, I believe it is good for you. It can help you.

It is amazing that there are people that have died a long time ago and it feels like they died just now. When you remember them, you only have to think of the pain and it comes back to you. Your fear of it is very great, so great it begins to transcend time. You don't know whether if it is now or if it was twenty years ago because your attachment to that soul in its physical form is so strong, and if you feel that once they are not longer in the physical and they are no longer around, you cannot enjoy their presence anymore.

If it is a parent and you feel they are not there with you to celebrate your new family or children, if it is a friend you feel that you can no longer enjoy the conversations or meaningful happy moments with them, I understand this. Some of you have had experiences where these people who have died - we say "crossed over" - have come to you in your dreams. You have seen signs. Amazing things have happened in your life, maybe not many, but a few. Do you ignore these signs?

There are so many books and stories about people who have received signs from their loved ones from who have crossed over. Beautiful stories. Do you choose to look the other way from these things? You can have these things happen in your own life. You don't have to feel such strong pain about the death of those loved ones.

Dealing with death is one of the hardest things you can do as a human being. How do you change something that is so strong in your consciousness? You can perhaps start to think about changing the way you think about death. See it as a transformation. See it as a new journey that the soul is embarking on. And see it as a release of your spirit into infinite love, glory, and peace. See it is as another level of education. For indeed it is.

Many of you feel that when you cross over all the work is done, that you will sit in Heaven and all your needs and your desires will be catered to, you will see all your loved ones, and you will be in glory infinitely. Really? Think about that for a moment. For eternity you will get everything you want and desire and need. It is like a vacation, an eternal vacation. Think about your vacations on the planet. You go away for a few days or maybe a week or a month. You experience all that fun and everything you desire and get…nonstop enjoyment.

What about that feeling that happens when you get tired? It happens all the time. You cannot stay on vacation very long. If you were to get stuck on a beautiful resort somewhere, that heavenly vacation can turn into hell because you want to go home to your busy troubled life. So it is not in your nature to have an eternity having certain dreams and desires satisfied. It is in your nature actually to constantly grow, learn, and experience.

That is what happens when you cross over to the other side. You still learn. Whether you call them "spirit guides" or "angels," I don't care, we are here. You sit with us in wonderful classes and you learn. You will see people you know and some you don't know, that are connected to you through your soul: Soul mates.

So why is there reincarnation? It is because you wanted to experience everything. You wanted to experience being a different person on the planet. You wanted to experience being rich, poor, strong, weak, healthy, weak, ill, having a short life, having a long life, being happy, being depressed, having a big family or dying alone. You choose it.

Many of you will say, "How can you choose to be born and suffer an illness and die at a young age of four? That is cruel, that is ungodly, and that is absurd." What are the facts you are going to use to base your opinions on? You only have one. And that is pain is wrong and suffering is wrong. That is the only thing you have to base your opinion on this teaching. It is because you don't believe, you don't believe that the soul is something greater than you can realize. But if you are truly a seeker, you are going to have to open your mind on this one to make yourself a more complete soul on your journey.

The people around you, they also are a part of this desire. They wanted to experience you in this particular lifetime, whatever interaction was going to happen. Some of you will say, "Red Eagle, are you saying every single thing was destined to happen and it was simply destined to happen? Then life is just a game played by some Creator for their own whims to watch us suffer on this planet, to watch us suffer in a destiny we cannot escape?"

That is not how it is at all. Nothing is predestined. Let me use the school analogy again. If you want a degree, don't you pick the best school that you can get into to help you get that degree? Are the courses not set? But you get to choose how you do in the course. Don't you have other students who are taking the same course, some who you don't know, some who you know? You meet there in that school and you do your best.

The only difference that I am saying is that there is some kind of psychic connection between all of you, all of your friends and family, all of the people that you meet. Before you were born you decided you were going to go to this school, "Planet Earth." There are souls in other cities and countries and you will meet them as time goes on.

You all planned this together, but you did not know exactly what was going to happen. Nobody did. So you do have free will, completely, because you also chose to come to this school.

There are other schools in other dimensions, in other systems, in other planets. Some people on your planet called "psychics," "mediums," "channels," they know about these other realms. Some of you have experienced that in your dreams. When you dream, you travel and see people whom you did not know. I know something many of you have experienced, like when you dream, you say to a friend, "Hey you were in my dream, but you were not you. I was in my house, but it was not my house."

Ha! I got you! You have experienced other dimensions. Right now I am trying to give you an explanation, so listen. You chose the parents you were born to, the place, the country, and certain key people who were going to help you with the kind of training, spiritual education, so you can get your degree.

What is your degree? It is another level of expansion, another level of expansion for your soul. It is not a reward that the Creator gives you. The reward is the *process itself.* The gift is the *journey itself.* And yet so many of you are not satisfied with society and the life system on this planet. You say, "This is crazy, get me outta here. Beam me up Scotty!" or "Let me find my purpose."

Get you out of here? So then why not go kill yourself. *What?* Was that too heavy for you? Yeah, I am telling you go kill yourself if you want to get out of here, but you won't do it. Do you want to know why? Because you do want to stay here, because there is a lot you like here, but somehow you convinced yourself that it is not enough. You are somewhere in between the idea that it should be much easier and it should be much harder.

It is so hard for you to enjoy life when you feel that you don't have a purpose or you don't know what your purpose is. Many of you go to a psychic and say, "What is my purpose?"

If the psychic says to you, "It is to enjoy your life fully," you are dissatisfied with that answer.

You want to hear: "Go to Africa and save the children." You want to hear: "Go to school and do that, and go accomplish this." You wait until you hear the perfect answer that resonates with your mood. You need somebody else to tell you because for some reason you, who have the purpose, don't know your purpose.

There could be a number of reasons you don't know your purpose. Maybe your ego is too big or maybe you don't have enough self-confidence. Maybe you created a set of circumstances in your life and experience that kept you busy for a long time, and you did not pay attention to your purpose because you were too busy trying to survive.

There are certain people who have been in thirty year marriages and their spouse dies or they get a divorce and children are grown, or they lose their job and suddenly they don't know what to do. The thought of rekindling their dreams that they once had is painful and seems unattainable.

Your purpose on the planet can change. I don't even like the word "purpose," but for the sake of this discussion I will use that word. Why can you not play music, and be a scientist, then be a monk, then be someone else? Why not be all of those things at once? That is actually better, to be all of those things at once. You place so many limits on yourselves, it is killing you every day. Slow death.

I can't paint a picture, I am not an artist, I cannot sing a song, I am not a singer. I cannot do this, I cannot do that. If an idea comes to you, if it is a song, sing it. If it is a poem, write it. If it is a meal, cook it. If it is a dance, dance it.

You don't have to be attached to the ideas that you are not a singer or a poet or a chef. You are a multi-dimensional vibrant being. Where you put your energy truly, truly, honestly, innocently, with hope and fire, you will blossom. It will sprout. It will bring you great satisfaction. And yet, "What is my purpose?" continues to plague you.

Some of the people on your planet who feel this way, they don't want to be here because it seems so elementary, seems so kindergarten because you are very far along on the metaphysical, spiritual path and you have been teachers. We understand, because your soul has a memory of being in certain dimensions where this kind of education is not part of the plan. It is a part of the process.

So there is some memory. The reason you have that is in a way to help keep you not too attached to this world and to be able to have some perspective. Because many of the people who need your help are so caught up. They don't have that perspective of, "This world is crazy, get me out of here, it is so silly." Some of them have the perspective, "I hate this world, get me out of here." That is a different.

Some of the spiritual teachers out there, the ones we call "Light Workers" - their perspective is the world seems that it is too silly, that people don't change their spots (like with a leopard). You are free. And you can appreciate this sentiment. *It does not need to be a burden to you.* Just live the free life that you are aware that you can live. Although you came to be a teacher, even you have to learn the lessons of this planet Earth, this existence and this incarnation. Everybody gets something out of this school. Some of the kids in the class are more advanced than some kids. That does not mean that you cannot enjoy the class if you are advanced or too behind. That is part of releasing the judgments on yourself - part of letting the ego die.

A word of solace and peace to all of you who have experienced loved ones crossing over. Know that every single one of your loved ones is doing okay, in fact they are doing much better! They are not dead. They are very much alive. They are experiencing more and more and more. Someday when you leave your physical body, my words will be proven true to you. In some ways there's no way I can prove it to you right now. I can only put it in these books for history from the other side.

Your loved ones are only a thought away. Oftentimes when you are feeling the saddest, they are right there. Sometimes you are going about your day and it creeps up on you, the memory - the painful memory - the death of your loved one, and you feel so alone.

My friends, when it suddenly creeps up on you, it is because the spirit of your loved one, they are around you at that very moment and you choose to believe that they are not! We want you to know, when you are feeling that pain that is the exact time to talk to them. The joy of knowing that person, you will always know that person. All of them on the other side want you to enjoy your life, this physical life, and then you will enjoy the life that you have after you leave this physical body. So hard to believe, isn't it? The fear of death is forced upon you from many cultures.

Some of your soul mates are not the person that you have a romantic relationship with. Then there are those souls that travel with you through many lifetimes, whether or not you believe in reincarnation, for this discussion is important. Whoever you met in this life, was a soul mate. Some will still be there after they cross over with you on the other side. For you all chose to learn these lessons together. You don't hold pain when you cross over - physical or emotional. You will not miss those who are still on the planet, though you will still love them. You will have a different perspective and you will see that there is no such thing as death.

It is like you are in one party and you leave and you go to another party in another part of the town. You are waiting for those who are still at the old party, to come to the new one. I have seen many souls cross over that did not believe what I am saying, and when I talk to them it is like they are slapping their foreheads and saying, "Oh, my God, why didn't I listen?" *Ha!* They are relieved of their regret.

Any shock or regret about dying is very momentary, and suddenly they are refreshed and rejuvenated with great support and understanding and compassion. They realize their journey is continuing.

Oftentimes what they feel what Heaven is like on the other side, they create. Yes, you can create your Heaven on the other side. Because if you cross over and to you Heaven is an amusement park, and to another person Heaven is like a rock concert or something like that or a quiet lake, it cannot be one Heaven for everybody. You are still a unique personality, soul essence. Heaven is created according to what you like! You don't have to take this information, but you can consider it as an option.

All of the religions, all of the traditions still are pointing to the light. They are not pointing to the darkness. Do you know that there are people on your planet that still remember their past lives? You don't read much about it, but there are many books and documented by researchers, and psychologist, therapist of all kind.

There are certain people who under hypnosis can remember their past lives, and can give details about the country and the place they have never been to, nor have been interested in. Even little children, they gave specific names, even addresses, and experiences that they remember from a past life and the parents were bewildered when they heard their child talking about it. They researched it and found out it was true.

So you can ignore all of that information if you want, and you will be ignorant. Is your ignorance bliss now that you have proof that there is evidence of past lives? For those of you who already believe in reincarnation and you are obsessed thinking about what you were, and who you were, and how it affects this particular life - if that information is revealed to you, you can look into it. But to constantly be thinking about what you did in a past life and who you were, to figure out this life…this vital life that you are experiencing now, is a waste of breath.

Some of you still wish you were living that past life in another place. Let me tell you something. All of your past lives are connected psychically, and all of those people you were in those past lives, they put all of their energy together to come back through time and space to *become you now.* They are looking to you! You don't need to look to them. They wanted to be you, to experience what you are experiencing now. Your past lives, it is like they are in the audience, and you are in the playing field, and they are cheering you on - thousands of them. You have been a woman and man, an old person, a child. You have been every nationality and religion. You have died young, you have died old, you have been murdered, and you have murdered.

It makes no sense for you to be prejudice of any kind in this lifetime. It makes no sense for you to identify so much with the culture you come from or the religion you come from. It was only this one time, more than likely. Stop always identifying yourself that you are from here or there. That keeps you from being here now. Do not ride on the coattails of your ancestors, to be so proud of what your people have done. What have you done? Your ancestors should be grateful and proud of themselves, for they are the ones who did it. What did you do? What are you doing? What traditions are you beginning? What legacy are you leaving behind?

This country, America, it is a very interesting place because so many people come from so many other places to do things here. As you say: "To go from nothing all the way to the highest something." It is possible here. It is a very unique and interesting experiment to create a culture from very many cultures.

Even though all of these people come from all of these different places, they still bring their fear of death with them. You are so afraid to leave this physical life. Indeed it is beautiful, pleasurable, fascinating, incredible, but there is more. Actually when you accept that there is more - more learning, more experiences, more love - then you can enjoy this place even more.

If you are at a party and the entire time you are looking at your watch, how can you enjoy the party? If you are always looking at your watch, you will be nervous at the party and you will not be able to experience it, enjoy others, the conversation, and the music, all that is new. Your body will begin to react also, for the body is always reacting to the mind, and the preoccupation of the mind. It is like this in life. Many people who hear that, create illnesses. Not all. Some. Maybe you find it hard to digest. It is a pretty heavy topic. And as the years go on I will communicate more to you on this subject and you will begin to understand more. But, for this chapter in this book, I want you to try to understand more and more that death is not separate from life. It is still life. It is a reorganizing, rejuvenation, a reset.

Your fear of death holds you back from living fully. You may say, "But Red Eagle, I know people who are living it up, going here, there, living every moment to the fullest. Partying hard, working hard, playing hard." Perhaps they are running, perhaps they are trying to squeeze everything in before they die. Perhaps it is exactly the opposite - that they are so full of fear of death, they are trying to squeeze everything in and looking as though they are truly loving life, talking very loud, laughing very loud, what they call "living out loud." They feel they are living more full lives than perhaps a fisherman in a village in some third-world country who is simply netting fish every day feeding his small family, not knowing how to read or write.

Who is living a more full life? We don't know. Do you want to know why? Because it is from the person's feeling deep within their souls, and that is hard to know because so many people are not honest about it. They do not live their truth. And when you do not live your truth, it is the ultimate slow death.

There are some of you who cannot wait to leave the planet because you think this a place of suffering. You say, "It is too dense here. I have to work too hard to create, to manifest." And it seems silly, yeah, in one respect it does seem silly to us that one of the main concerns for everyone on the planet is to pay rent. It is such a big concern for most of you. Every day you work so hard to make money to make sure you have a place to live. Then everything else comes after that. From a certain perspective, how silly does that seem?

You spend a third of your life sleeping, and most of your waking life worrying about the rent. Even if you are rich you still are concerned maintaining what you have, are you not? Many of you believe it is so much easier on the other side. Many of you believe it is a vacation from having to manifest and to create.

I will tell you something. Whatever patterns, challenges, issues that you have right now - when you don't clear them - they are still there on the other side. Some of you right now are saying, "Oh, no! Existence sucks. There is no escape." Yeah there is. Do you want to know? Your physical death is not the escape. The death of the ego is.

The death of the ego - I will have to explain that to most of you - because most of you feel the ego refers to the part of you that thinks you are better than everybody else. You say, "He or she is so egotistical." That is kind of a new definition. There is a spiritual definition that I will talk to you about. The ego is what keeps you from being truly free. It is your judgments on yourself and others. It is your lack of compassion toward yourself and others. It is your fear from going inside your own wounds to cleanse them and to heal them. It is your fear of going into other's wounds to assist in healing and cleansing. It is your fear of the unknown. It is the part of you that wants your life to improve, but not to change. But if it improves, it must change. It must die to bring in new life.

Chapter Twelve
The Body

It is said that if you do not have your health, you do not have anything. It doesn't matter how much money you have, or success. When you don't have your health, physical, mental, or spiritual – when these are out of balance nothing is right.

So far in this book we have talked about mental, spiritual, but not so much physical. There is nothing more complex and fascinating than the way a physical body moves through life, processing calculations – the solutions it finds are greater than any computer on your planet. A computer cannot feel. The human body take material, resources from the Earth, and transform them into a different kind of energy. Everything that comes out of the ground is fed by the sun. In your school they teach you a system – photosynthesis – taking the energy of the sun, the soil, the water, the wind and from that, it grows.

From the trees, the vine, the bush, the garden – out of the soil comes the things to replenish your body. Very simple and you know all of this. But the way your body takes the nutrients from the Earth, the sun, from the fruits, from the vegetables – that process is kind of a mystery to you – you and the doctors just accept that it happens.

Somebody tells you that this fruit has a particular vitamin in it, a mineral, and you eat it. That is all you have to do. Somehow your body knows what to do, and where it is supposed to go, and the part it does not need, it push out. How does it know? How does the body know what to do? How does every organ in the body know what to do? Each has a specific job. It is very amazing, there are so many people walking around not knowing what the different parts of their body do. They don't teach you that. You have to go to special school to learn that. If you use common sense in creating a society, you would say that is very important for people to know about their bodies. That is the vehicle they travel in for the rest of their lives!

Through that they feel everything. Through the body they interact with the world, so that should be of very, very high importance to you as a people. Not when it is too late and you ask your government to take care of you and to help you pay for your drugs. It is causing a strain on the entire world because you don't know how to take care of your bodies.

True, you know how to feed them, and how to wash them, and in the meantime try not to get killed. That is the most you do, and the people who are trying to do something better for themselves and for the world you call them "health nuts." They are crazy to you. Really? *They* are crazy because they care and they are trying to learn about what is good for them, and they are trying to stick to it? So they may be healthier and live better lives, so their children will be healthier and live better lives?

Are they the nuts or are *you?* You, who will go on continuing to put anything into their bodies, overeating the flesh of dead animals, of fruits and vegetables that have been tainted by poisons by companies who do not care anything about you, other than your money. By not moving your body, not exercising, by not doing the thing that your body is very good at: running, jumping, dancing, and moving. Over-eating the wrong things, over drinking the wrong things.

You are much more intelligent than that. But what has happened to many people is that your tastes and your sense of taste have become distorted. It is not your fault. Your society has changed and moved away from what is natural and good, and toward that which is too sweet or too salty, and what has been packaged and put on the shelves. That is not food. That is only something to put in your stomach to make the hunger go away.

When your body is balanced, there is a sensation that moves through it. It's like an electrical current. It is not too strong - it is steady, it is radiant, and it feels good. Stretching your body is like stretching your mind. It can only do good things for you. That we will talk about a little bit later. First I need to continue to talk about food. The incredible capabilities of your organs, including your brain that manages all those organs, is tremendous.

Every part of your body talks to the other part of the body, has to communicate. It cannot be that your liver lives there in your body and not communicate with your spleen and your pancreas, your heart, and your stomach. It has to know. It has to have some idea what is happening in its world. It has to live in harmony with each other.

Many of you are at war with your bodies, you want to overwork it, overstress it. You feel that the body should take a beating and that old age, and the weaknesses, and diseases, and struggles physically that are associated with it, are natural. Now in your country sixty years is old. There was a time "old" did not begin until ninety years in many civilizations. Look around you. You don't have to believe Red Eagle. How many radiant, healthy, happy beings are you seeing?

Next time you are in the market, look who is smiling, who is standing up straight and strong, who is not overweight, who is not buying medicines all the time? The facts are in front of you. The health of your body is in your hands. You can have that electricity running through you. Instead of dulling it down and covering it with layers of bad food, covering it with poisons, toxins that is found everywhere.

You have to keep the basics in your life very strong. Red Eagle not saying it is bad to have ice cream, things that are fun to eat. But your basics must be solid. You would never think to put Coca-Cola® into your car instead of gasoline, would you? It would not run. Maybe you can put it into the radiator because that takes water, but still that is poison water you are putting in there if you put soda into the radiator of your car.

Your body is so beautiful, it is so beautifully adaptive, that it begins to accept the bad things you put into it, and try to extract anything good that is left there. And that takes a very long hard toll on the body and that is why you age prematurely. Eat more foods that are alive, not dead. Flesh that you eat of the animals is dead. Try to limit that. Do you not care about the animals?

When you eat the flesh of the animals, even your doctors have said to you to cut it down but you don't want to. It tastes too good for you and it is too easy to get. The companies that put it out there for you to make it easy to eat, they don't care about the quality because you are burning it, putting it in the microwave, and radiating your food so that anything that was alive in your food is dead. So what are you eating? Rotting flesh. There is no nutrition in there, but they put a lot of salt and the sugar and other things in there, and you eat it because it is affordable and easy to get.

The fruits and vegetables – they have lost their flavor because you have destroyed the soil. They do not taste good anymore. Your children do not want to eat an apple because it is not sweet to them. There are two things that are happening. One is that you have destroyed the soil for the apple like it used to be, like in the time of Red Eagle. Oh! You would eat an apple and you would taste like there was sugar in there! The other thing is that you have ruined the taste buds of your children. They are very tiny and you are giving them very super sweet things to drink and so in comparison, nothing is sweet anymore. It is a double whammy.

You have to re-train yourselves. Sorry to say it and I am sure you are sorry to hear it, but you don't *want* to re-train yourself. You will listen to anything about the mind but you don't want to hear too much about the body. You don't want to be told what you should eat and what not eat, because it feels too good to eat whatever you want. You have been bombarded with lies about food and when certain people on the Earth will try to tell you the truth about the food, you think they are nuts.

Why don't you give them a chance to speak? Why don't you try to listen to what they are saying? They are saying all of those things so that people can feel better on the planet. They are tired of so many people are dying, getting diseases and are getting sick. Think of how many people are in your family now that have diseases and conditions that are making you sad. Sad to see them like that, sad to see their suffering. Now everybody has to take care of them, and yourself.

The medicines are expensive, the whole system, is this too much for you to hear, that everything is so bad, that everything you eat is poisoning you? Or is that your logic to escape this type of understanding and say, "To hell with it, I will die when I die?" Is that what you will tell your children or the ones who love you? Or are you giving in when you know a better way, and a better way is available to you?

Is that what you have become, so stuck in your ways, *huh?* That even if it kills you prematurely and the pain you are suffering, you don't care as long as you don't have to change your ways? You can change your ways. You can get back to the basics and still enjoy your life. In fact you will enjoy your life more.

They are now creating medicines for everything. If you move your leg too much, there is a medicine for that! Maybe they will come up with something even more crazy soon, and they do not tell you the truth about those drugs, the side effects. They have to put it in tiny little letters on the label. They create medicines to make you happier, because you won't do anything about it, like work on your emotions by meditating or taking responsibility. So pay them and they will give you something, a legal drug to make you high to distract you from the things in your life that you should work on.

And guess what? These anti-depressants, *one of the side effects is you want to kill yourself.* That is how much you have been fooled.

Think about it. You are sad and you don't want to live anymore, so you take anti-depressants and *the anti-depressants can make you want to kill yourself.* Do you know how many people have already killed themselves that were taking anti-depressants that did not want to kill themselves before? Do they tell you that in your newspapers or magazines? No, because the people who own the magazines also own the medicines, but you don't want to know. It is kind of a doom's day prophecy for you. *It does not have to be.*

You spend your money on many things that do not help you. But you could spend your money on things that can help you to eat in a more natural way, the organic way. Eating fruits and vegetables that have not been tainted with poisons, chemicals, pesticides that are hurting your children, you believe they have the power, but money is power!

How you spend your money is where the power is. You can take away their power tomorrow. You refuse to buy what they sell. Then you will see perhaps who is the power. They will crumble within a few months. They will go crying and running to the government to help them. You should care more about your health and your children's health and the ones whom you love – their health – more than the about the profits of these big companies.

Now is the time, because of your Internet, that you have more access to all of the information that you need. You have no more excuses that you don't know. It is so hard to change this one aspect of your life that you spend billions of dollars trying to figure out how to lose weight, when there are only two ways: Eat less and to move your body more. Nothing else.

You don't need to read a book on how to lose weight. You need to read two sentences. Here they are again: Eat less. And move your body more. You don't know what to eat? Eat what comes out of the ground from the trees and plants. That is your answer. Now, if you don't want to do that, that is your own problem, but don't say you don't know how. Use your common sense, but because you don't want to use your common sense, the animals are suffering.

My people, in the winter months when there was no food that was growing out of the ground, we would kill buffalo and other animals. We did not overeat them and we did not torture them. We tried to take their life as fast as we can. For you see, the animals are sharing the planet with us. They are our brothers and sisters. There is a divine connection between Heaven and Earth...the circle of life.

Other times we eat the grains, the fruits, the berries, the vegetables, the corn. We were very strong, we would drink clean water from the streams with minerals, and we were very healthy and we moved our bodies. We danced, and sang, and chanted. But the animals, so many of them are being killed every day.

Polluting your land, soil, your streams. Wasting so much energy, and on top of that not giving you the best health, giving you diseases of the heart, cancers, all of these different things.

You have to learn moderation. I am not talking about extreme lifestyles – it is not for everyone. I know that your society will not become a vegetarian society. But you are consuming *too much meat.* All animal diet? What happened to you? You used to care about the animals when you were a child. If someone was hurting an animal it was an outrageous crime to you. You would rush to help that animal. You would tell a grown-up. You would try to comfort the animal. *Animals were your friends.* Now you don't care as long as you get to eat them.

That is the truth. You can deal with it or don't deal with it. I am only offering you an option of moderation if you are going to consume them for your food. The health of your world will improve.

What about as you are eating your food? What are the thoughts going through your mind before you eat it? In many cultures you say a prayer before you eat. I like this very much. If you are religious or not religious, it is good to be thankful for the food you are eating. You can thank God, the Universe, Mother Nature, whatever, or even the person who sold it to you. I don't care. But be thankful.

Do you know you can put beautiful, happy, emotional energy into your food? That was the whole point when you were saying prayers before you ate. Because when you said the prayer or the blessings or expressed the gratitude, that feeling create a vibration. That vibration is directed toward the food, and the food absorbs that vibration.

Why do you think Grandmother's food tasted better than anybody else's? Because she loved you and was happy to do it and that got into her food, and then your system. Many people will agree to this, they will say, "Yeah, you can taste the love."

I am talking about the *feelings* - your *feeling* connection to food. Forget the scientist right now; they don't have a machine to measure the love in the food. *Ha!* If they do not have a machine to measure it, they do not believe it is real. You don't need a machine to measure your feelings, connections to that which is life and all that warms your soul.

All meals are best shared, are they not? When you receive a plate of food, no matter what the food is, be grateful. Take one moment at least to pause, to place your hands above the food, and connect with a good feeling inside of yourself to help cleanse the food, to put better energy into your body. Maybe the person next to you will think you are a little crazy, *huh?* Putting your hands above the food, sending vibrations into it, they will think you are nuts, *huh?* They will think you are becoming one of those health nuts. But you know what? Maybe if you explain it to them, they might be a little open minded.

You see, you have to have guts. You have to stand up for something that perhaps you can believe in. Stop running away from what people will think about you. What are you anyway? Are you a human being that follows common sense? Are you a person who is on this planet to become better in body, mind, and spirit, or are you not? Do you think you know everything?

The body is a temple. The act of eating can be a divine action. It is the ultimate in recycling! It comes out of the Earth, you eat it, take what you need from it, and what you don't need your body pushes it out, excrete it out; it is used as fertilizer in the soil for more food to grow. *Ha!* That is how smart nature is. It can even take your waste, add a seed, and grow food out of it. I wonder if you will ever be as intelligent.

I wonder if you ever realize that you *are* as intelligent. You are not separate from your body, you are one with it. You don't own it, you dwell within it, and yet you are also it.

How you think, how you feel, it affects your body. Your body stores pain, stores memories of pain in your muscles, in your joints, in different muscles in your body. It is not common for a person in your society to get a massage. In most of the world, no, but in the cultures where massage is more a part of daily life you have more calm, more balanced, healthier physically and emotionally.

It is simple. You feel better when you are touched. If you bang your knee in your house walking around, why do you rub it? You feel better if you do. You don't know why that is happening, or how it works...you just know that if you rub it, it feels better. Many people when they get massages, memories start to come up that they forgot about, usually painful ones because it is being stored in the body. Too much stress and your neck and your shoulders begin to tense up and it becomes very hard, or your hips, or your back or your face – anywhere in the body. It is good to make massage a part of your life. You say you cannot afford it. Learn it, get a book. Massage your family member or your friend. You can practice together. These are simple practical things I am telling you.

Do you want to feel better or you don't? I know you do. I am giving you simple ways. Many people cannot afford these things. I say can you not afford not to do it? Because sooner or later it will catch up with you and you will become ill. Then you will not be able to work and make money and other people will have to take care of you and you will lose many things. The prevention is the best cure.

Be good to your body. Do not rush through the bathing ritual when you are taking a shower. Don't rush. Take some time. You have that peace. Many of you have children and busy lives. The only time you have alone is in the shower, so make the most of it. Feel the water cleansing the body like it is cleansing the soul. Relax the body, and see negativity being washed away down the drain. It is a kind of meditation. It is very good for the people who do not meditate. At least when they are in the shower it removes any negative feelings, the ritual of bathing. It is time alone to find peace.

What about preparing your own food instead of going outside to get it? You say it is too time consuming, why? What else do you have to do? Take care of your children? Why are they not learning to cook? Why do you not make them sit in the kitchen and watch you? Are they too out of control? Maybe it is from all the sugar you are feeding them. You have to put your foot down and make a change.

Perhaps you are single, alone, and it makes you feel sad to cook for yourself – nobody there to share it with you. When you cook for yourself, you are taking care of yourself, you start to feel better. When you feel better, you get happy and when you are happy, you attract love into your life, more friends, and a romantic relationship, and you are not alone. So don't cut yourself off at the knees and say you cannot cook for yourself because you are alone. It is a way of nurturing yourself.

Slow down the pace a little bit. When it is time to move quickly and fast in your life, it will be enjoyable and you will do so. Make your health your priority. Make a few changes. I am not asking you to change everything all at once. But start to make some changes.

When you are feeling sick, do not keep telling yourself that you are sick. It delays the process of healing. Say to yourself: *I am healing.* Lie in your bed and say it in your mind that you are healing. Feel the healing energy of the light moving through your body.

Do you know even doctors in hospitals are telling their patients to think more positively, even to meditate, and feel that things are getting better, and to laugh more? They are aware that how the person feels emotionally is going to help them physically. You may look in the mirror and say: *I am going to lose weight, I am losing weight.* But your subconscious looks in the mirror and keep telling yourself that you are fat, tired, and lazy.

But your conscious mind is repeating over and over and over again that you are going to lose weight, but your subconscious mind is running the show. You have to go into that part of you that says: *Yeah, I feel bad about myself, but I will make a change. I am going to tell those negative emotions to calm down and get out of the driver's seat.* They may still be in the car with you but at least they are not driving the car. The positive emotions are driving the car.

Sooner or later the negative emotions will get tired and they will go to sleep, and you can enjoy the rest of your journey reconnecting with the incredible life force that you are.

Chapter Thirteen
The Beginning

There is a famous line from a famous book that says, "In the beginning, there was the Word." From that Word, everything came into being. Are you a person of your word? Can you tell what and who you are from your word? That shows us how you are "being." In this life it is said that if you don't stand by your word, you don't have anything.

When you want to begin a new life, you must say it to yourself. You must say the word and the word is: *Yes. Yes* to life, *yes* to possibility, *yes* to hope, *yes* to love, *yes* to the world, *yes* to yourself. That everything that you ever dreamed was possible for your life is possible. But it seems in your lives, you are more concerned with endings than beginnings. You fear endings, you worry about endings. Nobody likes to say good-bye.

This last chapter is not "good-bye," my friends. This is "hello." We have begun a journey together. Think of your life as a relationship, a mad passionate love affair with everything with your world. That when you were born, you came into this life as the beginning of a love affair, a love affair that had taken you into other worlds within your heart, within your mind.

The places you have been, the things that you have seen, are so deep and so intriguing. Everyone that is alive on your planet, some point on their journey has experienced love, magic, surprise, and change.

This is the nature of your existence in this lifetime. How you conduct yourself, carry yourself through this amazing journey, is important. Your flexibility, your balance, your passion, and your compassion, your strength and your vulnerability, your intelligence and your naiveté – all of these things are required to have a fulfilling life experience.

You travel through your life and you meet your tribe, others like you. You call them your friends, those who believe in the same things you believe in, and same things you hope for; ones who feel empathy and sympathy between each other. They say you cannot choose your family, but you chose your friends. You have chosen your family as well. You chose them before you were born, before you began. You chose the family you have because you wished to know intimately people you would chose to not associate with otherwise, and perhaps even to love them.

So why did you chose this world? It wasn't to hate or disconnect with everyone. You came here to connect, you came here to share, and you came here to create, not to destroy. You came here to begin. In your understanding, you believe that if there is a beginning, there must be an ending. And with endings you associate with mostly sad feelings: *It was the end of an era, the marriage that was once beautiful ended, the friendship that was once bountiful and joyous ended...the party was over and we had to go home.*

But there is no death. There is no end. You are eternal beings. There is a love for you that we have as we watch over you and work with you, that if you were to feel this love in its entirety you could not bear it. We know who you are. Do you?

What I have said to you in this book, was not said to you because you are wrong and that you have been bad in some way. The messages that I am delivering to you, the lessons I am trying to share with you, are because you are my friends and there is no other reason.

We only wish to awaken you like a good friend who would awaken a friend who is sleeping through the best part of the movie. *Hey! Wake up, you are missing something. You can sleep later.*

And when you receive these messages, share them like taking one candle and lighting the other candle with it - and that candle and another and so on. And each candle, millions of them, billions of them, shining their light. And yet no candle holds a flame that is brighter than the other.

The light is the teachings; you hold that light like a candle. And if you blow out, there are others that can help re-light you. That is what friends do, that is what human beings should do. Not to blow each other out and shove each other out of the way. There is enough sunshine for everyone. If you go to the beach on a sunny day, you don't have to push people out of the way to get sunlight. There is plenty of sunshine for everyone. Everyone you meet is trying to get that light somehow, so do not fight with them. Help them to see there is enough room for everyone. That way you don't have to end anything and you are always creating new beginnings. You don't have to worry about the past and the future.

Think of your lives as a symphony, as an orchestra. Think of your lives as a beautiful piece of music played by an orchestra that is comprised by many different singers and many different sounds. The sounds in the instruments represent the different people of the Earth. With all their different personalities, colors, textures, cultures, there is a sound that is created from the energy of the people of the Earth and all the animals. And we can tell you that we can hear it, the song of your existence.

Do you think about your planet? I know some of you are really into taking care of the planet. To save the planet you do many good things, many good deeds, and we are happy about that. What would be a very good thing for you to do is to spend maybe one full minute a day sending love to the planet.

All you have to do is to picture the Earth floating in front of you like a beach ball, and to love it and to send love to everyone on the planet, her oceans, and all of nature. To send love to your ancestors as well as to your descendants…to the people on the left and to the right and on the fence, wish peace for everyone, wish peace for *everyone*, wish peace for everyone. That is the song that you can create, with all of your fellow musician singers on the planet.

There was an explorer who was looking for the new world. He came to these shores in this land called America. He encountered my people. We regarded the Earth as our mother; the trees, the plants the wind, the river, as our siblings. For that explorer it was a new world - intriguing, beautiful, and at times frightening.

To us it was our normal everyday life, it was our world to us, not a new world. And those explorers who interacted with us learned many new things. And today many of the places in this particular land still has our names that we gave to it, and there are many spirits in those places.

Many conflicts with our people, there was much death and destruction, we lost many men, women and children, homes. Now many of those spirits from the native people are assisting spiritually people who are still on the planet. We do not hold anger, nor do we desire revenge. We hope that our legacy means something to people to return once again to the beginning, to return to integrity with yourself, with others, with our planet, our mother.

You can create a new world, you can begin, you can have your word mean something again, you can begin anew again, and you can be good again. May the dark night of the soul pass, let the morning breeze and light shine down on you, my friends. The only world that will end is the world of ignorance. And it will do you a world of good. Other than that, there are only beginnings. Bless you.

Riz Mirza

Riz has given countless personal psychic readings all over the world as well as teaching workshops. With roots in India and New York City, Riz lives with Oriah in Los Angeles, California. He still writes and sings songs and paints.

www.RizMirza.com

Oriah Miller

Oriah is a global resource for empowering mothers and women. She is an accomplished producer of two TV and film production companies. She is the founder of Women Without Borders US and an author.

Oriah has overcome domestic violence and has raised five successful children. A former police officer and current holistic healer and Life Coach, she teaches women and mothers how to manifest their dreams in one-on-one coaching and workshops, Twin Flame workshops, and Death of the Ego-Spiritual Rebirth coaching. She lives with her partner, Riz Mirza, in Marina del Rey, CA.

www.OriahLifeCoaching.com

Riz Mirza Channeling Chief Red Eagle

Several years ago a remarkable phenomena began to occur in the life of psychic medium Riz Mirza. While in deep meditation, he began psychic communication with Red Eagle. Red Eagle called himself a "spirit guide" whose intention was to deliver messages of love, wisdom, insight, and humor. Chief Red Eagle appeared in the form of a wise Native American elder warrior. He offered to speak through Riz the way a musician would express through an instrument. These "songs" would be dedicated to people everywhere. Thus, Red Eagle began his work speaking to small audiences in Los Angeles and then on to many countries around the world. *Red Eagle Speaks* is a gift of love and assistance. The gift of understanding yourself and others is now and has always been in your hands.

What People Are Saying About Red Eagle, Riz, and the Channeling Gatherings

I am stunned by the perception and love with which Red Eagle approached me during the group session. No one knows what he knew about me in an instant of flashing eyes. I am planning to follow up on his brilliant suggestions.

— Kenyon Taylor, RCST, natural medical intuitive, Ojai, CA

I am still feeling the energy from your gathering in Sherman Oaks last night...I feel profoundly touched...what came through for me.....every single word of it gave me so much clarity into my life and my own spirit. This was my first time ever hearing my spirit guides speak to me in this direct way through Red Eagle...and along with the clarity from them, he showed so much compassion and love for me and my life...it made me want to cry...sitting in Red Eagle's presence I felt translucent...even when I didn't ask one question, he even brought to my attention something I was not bringing up. It left me with such a deep feeling of relief from some answers, and others brought me a deep soul level assurance for my life and what I am here to do. Thank you for being who you are that you allow this divine work to happen through you. My soul feels FREE today...with a huge expansion in my heart... AND I honestly have never thought about archangels before.... but this morning...somehow I was very aware of Metatron...who I had never heard of before at all. I am so excited for MORE!

— Ava Violette Laurel, Sherman Oaks , CA

I have only just been introduced to Red Eagle this past two weeks. There are no words to describe the growth I have had in two weeks. I have been working on me for years. I do not feel like I am the same inside. Red Eagle brings his messages with nothing else but pure love. I feel more clarity, and more understanding of how I have been 'doing my life' all these years. I have some issues with my mom and last week I had a beautiful conversation with her. I actually spoke my truth and Red Eagle has brought this to my attention. We all try to hide our hurts and things that we do not want to look at but when we look at all the hurts and bring them into the open, we can than start to LIVE the life we all want. I am on the path of healing my relationship with my mom. I wish I could hang out with Red Eagle every day but if I close my eyes and listen to my heart and listen to my intuition I know he is always with me. Thank you Red Eagle for showing me how to live.

— Sandra Zislis, hairstylist, San Pedro, CA

Red Eagle is a really funny man who loves to get his point across with humor. He always relates current situations with a reference to his time on earth. He can easily connect with people very quickly and provides you with an accurate assessment of your abilities and what you stand for which earns his credibility within seconds. Red Eagle has provided me with validity to my current life transitional challenges and has confirmed my passions and integrity. I am excited that he is willing to share his messages with the rest of the world and give anyone a chance to open their minds to the universal teachings of a true legend and Native American chief with this book. I will definitely read it with a desire to apply it to my life.

— Chris Thompson, young entrepreneur with an MBA, Palm Springs, CA

I have been on a rollercoaster of a journey – seeing myself clearly -following the treasure map to get to the treasure. The message that he gave me helped me to let go of any remnants of doubt that I was having about the vision I see for myself '...the story I have been writing...' He could SEE me...I felt the love, comfort, and truth in his words... I am grateful for the opportunity in meeting him.

— Lisa Luera, Realtor®, San Pedro, CA

In this super-fast society in which we live - everyone seems to be longing for 'instant gratification' - ALWAYS with the base-intention that they will FEEL BETTER as a result of 'getting what they want'... the faster the better, but it's STILL about HOW they feel. We all judge virtually EVERYTHING in our lives based on 'how it will make us feel.' Well, when it comes to Red Eagle's wise insights and advice, whether in a live channeling or in print, all I can tell you is that Red Eagle's words always make me FEEL BETTER, because his words ALWAYS resonate in my Heart, where it COUNTS, where you "KNOW," versus "just believe" that important truths are now feeding a craving in your soul that you could never really quite explain. Just like the Sly & the Family Stone hit song of the late 1960s - Red Eagle's Divine Intent is ALWAYS - simply - "I Want to Take you Higher" ... and he DOES so - with GREAT skill. I know this - because, I can FEEL IT!

— Dennis Strahl, commercial metals-mines developer,
Goldfield, NV/ Palm Desert, CA

I was impressed by what Red Eagle had to say and with his mannerisms - he is such a joker, he likes a good laugh, and he really hits the point of what you need to hear. I have seen him countless times and have brought numerous friends to experience his wisdom and love. It's been a genuine pleasure to have seen Red Eagle and to know Riz, who with so much grace, allows him to speak through him.

—Therese Clinton, entertainment entrepreneur, intuitive,
Pasadena, CA

Riz is the light. There isn't any doubt about that whatsoever. One of the very first things he said to me in our test reading and interview - before I said one word - is that a situation I was concerned about was being taken care of and all was in process. And it was all resolved within the next few days, actually. A reading with Riz is one that you will want to savour. You hang up the phone with not only a whole different outlook and lots of information, but also with a whole different vibration.

— Dyan Garris, Voice of the Angels.com Psychic Network,
Sedona, AZ

"People ask what happens when they die, and I ask them what happens when you start to live?" ~Riz

To find a Riz Mirza channeling gathering near you or to request one in your city:

www.rizmirza.com
www.redeaglespeaks.com

Forthcoming Books by Riz Mirza

With a slate of books planned, Riz will be channeling various spirit guides as Oriah transcribes these books. Oriah is documenting the incredible messages and experiences, bearing witness to these extraordinary channeling circles held around the world.

Magical You
By Merlin

Merlin, the "master wizard," is a legendary figure whose energy and wisdom has been channeled beautifully by Riz over the years around the world. In this book, Merlin takes you on a journey to discover your truly magical, creative essence and how to renew your connection to the Universe.

Helen Speaks: How to See and Hear

Riz Mirza channels Helen Keller bringing forth messages on communicating with love and clarity and rising higher. As told to Oriah Miller.

Twin Flame Relationships: A Book of Love

Riz Mirza and his fiancé Oriah Miller explain the powerful relationship between Twin Flames and how it goes beyond Soul Mates. How to attract this type of relationship, what to do once you're involved and how it changes your life.

Red Eagle Listens

Chief Red Eagle returns with a book of questions fielded by the readers and answers in his inimitable fashion. Channeled by Riz Mirza as told to Oriah Miller.

Notes

Notes

Notes

Notes

Made in the USA
Lexington, KY
21 September 2011